Picnic Crumbs

A Gathering of Picnics,
Packed Lunches and Provisions
At Home and Abroad

Anabel Loyd

British Library Cataloguing in Publication Data.
A catalogue record for this book is available from the British Library.

ISBN 978-0-9570481-0-2

Published by
Polperro Heritage Press,
Clifton-upon-Teme, Worcestershire
WR6 6EN
United Kingdom
www.polperropress.co.uk

Printed in Great Britain by
Orphans Press, Leominster
United Kingdom

Contents

Foreword

Ah, the smell of it! Carcinogenic sausages being incinerated by Papa. Ah, the taste of it! Sand sandwiches with marmite and lettuce on the beach with Nanny. Ah, the grandeur of it! The sushi bars and cocktail mixologists in marquees now to be found at the ultimate picnic with bankers at the Fourth of June at Eton.

I am delighted that Anabel Loyd's enchanting and erudite treatise on picnic heaven has no truck with the latter. The perfect picnic summons up everything delightful about the outdoors: sunburn, a blinding wind, discomfort and probably the dog being sick. This is why the picnic is indispensable to the idiosyncratic British psyche and was an Empire-building endeavour. When the Good Lord divided the loaves and the fishes I cannot imagine that He thought the divine result would be an eternal sardine sandwich. Anabel, while espousing the sardine con brio, really glows when she introduces us to the picnics of yore à la Edward VII at the opera. Glyndebourne, Garsington and the Grange picnic competitors please note lobster mayonnaise, plovers' eggs, lamb cutlets, Parisian pastries and that "Gold plate was taken along as well to remind the King that it was a royal meal, even if it came from hampers".

Queen Victoria seems to have been ruthless at demanding passing peasants to boil water for her kettle in their cottages, so she and John Brown could have a cuppa, but at least she plonked her little round self in the heather. King George V and Queen Mary sat on upright chairs on the shores of Loch Muick while a ghillie set forth in a rowing boat to net brown trout. Loelia, Duchess of Westminster, recalls that "We gathered up the sliver slithering fish in buckets and took them to the chef who, in full regalia, white cap and all, was ready with a hot fire." The fish fry was then served by footmen and 'Was delicious as anything that I have ever tasted".

We know that our own dear Queen favours the burnt sausage but surely one of the many regrettable aspects of the decommissioning of the Royal Yacht *Britannia* is the loss of the picnic equipment list. During Her Majesty's summer cruise the boatswain was responsible for the landing arrangements for picnics with the appropriate equipment which included two tents, ground sheets, a shovel, gas lamps, blankets and 'Games (buckets, spades, balls)'. One feels rather more warmly towards Princess Margaret after discovering that her trips to the ballet or theatre would be followed by picnicky dinners: 'a cold chicken with lovely salads' or a 'picnic with steaks', details Anabel unearthed from Leo Groden's *My Royal Cookbook*.

Indeed, her research has been formidable. For most of us our acquaintance with Elizabeth David consists of *An Omelette and a Glass of Wine* but Anabel has dug deep to find David's description of the Maharajah of Jaipur's picnic in 1937 consisting of cold curry of boar's head (without the eyes) and a hamper of whisky.

I certainly can never resist the allure of P.G. Wodehouse and Anabel recalls young Bingo's paean to a picnic in *Jeeves and the Old School Chum*: "There's ham sandwiches," he proceeded, a strange, soft light in his eyes, 'and tongue sandwiches and potted meat sandwiches and game sandwiches and hard-boiled eggs and lobster and a cold chicken and sardines and a cake and a couple of bottles of Bollinger and some old brandy." "It has the right ring," Bertie said "And if we want a bite to eat after that, of course we can go to the pub."

Foreword

Picnic Crumbs is sprinkled with charming recipes – Coronation Chicken, Bloody Mary, Asparagus Rolls – that are balm to the soul, although I might pass on the udder sandwich. My personal picnic innovation is the wide-necked thermos – perfect for keeping new potatoes hot, buttery and minty to be eaten with Alderton ham marinaded in marmalade by Richard Craven-Smith-Milnes (available by post from Country Victuallers). What Anabel Loyd has achieved, with subtlety and gentle humour, is a chronicle of food fashion with a bracing whiff of the great outdoors. As the modern picnic sadly owes more to M&S, Prêt and the disposable barbecue than to Mrs David or Nanny, mistress of the egg sandwich, who does not long for curried boar's head?

Victoria Mather
London, May 2012

Picnic Crumbs

A Gathering of Picnics, Packed Lunches and Provisions at Home and Abroad

'I can recall in vivid detail the sense of freedom, the anticipation of meals that would be different, the feeling of summer heat as I stretched on the grass. Never has the whirr of a mowing-machine been so suggestive of holiday freedom. Going away for a youngster can be a crescendo of pleasures. They merge in a succession of joys. There is an unconscious retransfiguration of things both trite and commonplace. Somehow I always associate such reactions with picnic days. Picnic baskets have a spell of their own. Hard-boiled eggs are hardly a delicacy, yet they taste differently when eaten in the open air, particularly when the salt is produced in a screw of newspaper. Nobody wishes to devour sandwiches for ever, but it is remarkable how delectable two smeary pieces of bread encasing unappetizing cold beef can become. The meal has almost sacramental significance. As a connoisseur once remarked, the essential quality of a picnic is the doing of perfectly normal things in an abnormal place or manner. It is that quality that appeals so strongly to youth, the mental picture of adults squatting in a circle round baskets and glasses and bottles.'

(Louis T. Stanley, *The London Season*)

This book is for friends and family and especially for Heather, who taught me to make mayonnaise and made unsurpassable picnics; for Bobs, who took food very seriously, and for Mrs Macneil, who first allowed me to mess about in her kitchen.

I was inspired by two people who drew my attention to a contemporary gap in what I had thought to be an already crowded market. The first, a friend of my youngest daughter, eating her way through the home-made minced duck samosas, products of rather mixed Asian ancestry, that were part of a parents' day picnic last year, said: 'These are absolutely delicious, where did you get them?' The other, my eldest daughter's boyfriend, the artist Peter Haslam Fox, suggested a picnic book on the basis of my austerity family Christmas present, a small miscellany of Christmas snippets à la John Julius Norwich's *Christmas Cracker* and called 'Pudding Crumbs'. Fox thought that 'Picnic Crumbs' should be the next step and this latest effort is greatly improved by his whimsical and wonderful illustrations.

Introduction

'"The war is no picnic", someone will remark from time to time, and that phrase alone proves how high a place the picnic holds in man's affection. It offers through the generations a quiet and rustic ideal, attainable only during spells of utter calm, snatched from the world's restlessness and disillusion. Indeed a picnic resembles an essay in that its whole purpose is to afford pleasure; and it therefore seems appropriate that an essay, or part of one, should be dedicated to it ... Yet nobody I think, would pretend that it was other than an ugly word, picnic, verging on chit-chat or snip-snap ... It is, in fact, a busy, self-assertive, mediocre word that has sacrificed all dignity, but without attaining any compensatory sense of ease. Imagine the loss to us had Manet, for example, name his famous picture *Le Pique-Nique* instead of *Déjeuner sur l'Herbe*. Again, to eat *al fresco* sounds much more delightful than to picnic – but then it does not possess quite the same significance; to eat out-of-doors is not enough, otherwise the every snack of every tramp would constitute a picnic ... No, it implies – though this shade of meaning is contained in no definition of the word to be found in a dictionary – that one has a home and eats out-of-doors by choice.'

(Osbert Sitwell, *Picnics and Pavilions*)

Introduction

A book of picnics and picnic food is nothing new. There are manuals, the 'essential picnic recipes' with lists of foods for every outdoor occasion; volumes on picnics in art and literature, glossy with photographs and spiked with visually delicious recipes; chapters of information on intelligent picnic baskets and inspiring locations. The doyennes of cookery writing, Constance Spry, Elizabeth David, Claudia Roden, and others less widely known to casual cooks today, have beguiled their readers for a century or more with stories of picnics, their own and other people's, whetting appetites for outdoor eating, picnics and picnic foods from around the world. Using reminiscence as much as recipes they have created a sense of time and place, of convivial scenes, sunlight and unhurried pleasures to be treasured among other memories of busy lives. Their descriptions are punctuated with perfect recipes and the fruits of scholarly investigation into other and earlier food writers and those whom circumstances force to eat outdoors as well as true lovers of alfresco entertainments.

Picnic Crumbs too is a tally of memories, mostly other people's and occasionally my own. It revisits the work of innumerable food writers and descriptions of food and eating in less kitchen-orientated books and accounts that fit into the broad picnic category and somewhat, occasionally quite far, beyond. The selection is based on nothing at all beyond my enjoyment of a scene or the possibilities of the food conjured by the written description. My picnic memories range from the warmth of an Indian evening to a miraculously perfect summer interval at Glyndebourne or even scarcer days on the Scottish West Coast, where, from the rocks overlooking a white sand beach, a view of purple hills and glittering water to break your heart, make it the only place in the world to be. More typical is the squashed car interior in a wet car park waiting for some soggy school event when a good ham sandwich provides some small solace and may bring a greater optimism to lighten a dreary afternoon.

The Oxford Companion to Food summarises a broad selection of unsurprisingly unvarying definitions of the word 'picnic', mandatory to the introduction of any book on the subject. Preceded in the *Companion* by the mundane pickling onion, picnic is succeeded by piddock, an eatable of inspiring properties, capable of rendering luminous milk in which it is immersed, or breath if one is held in the mouth. Picnics can be as ordinary as the pickling onion or as magical as the luminescent piddock, a bacon sandwich on a suburban train or a perfect bento box, flower-viewing food, to be eaten as a pikunikku under the great cherry blossom canopies of the Japanese spring.

The late Alan Davidson, author of the *Companion*, writes: 'For many people, contemporary picnics involve an element of simplicity, where uncomplicated food such as hard-boiled eggs, sandwiches, pieces of cold chicken are eaten without ceremony.' True enough and this book has its fair share of hard-boiled eggs and sandwiches in humble settings besides more exotic and quixotic dishes eaten in less obvious situations.

Literary picnics and alfresco eating, whether fiction or fact, are inescapable, although the best known, such as Ratty's, do escape reiteration in these pages. Painted picnics appeal to the eye but there are difficulties in the successful identification of painted food that is only a small part of the composition or merely the titular excuse for a charming scene. Even at Tissot's beautifully painted picnics it hardly matters whether the cake is currant or sultana or the pie pork or game, the picnickers themselves are the point and likewise at a Brueghel peasant feast. I do, however, have an inherited painting of an Edwardian croquet game, with tea on the lawn, where the biscuits in the foreground are quite clearly Rich Tea; possible, as they were developed in Yorkshire as early as the 17th century.

Certain regional foods of the world are particularly transportable or otherwise suited to outdoor eating. Claudia Roden cites the dips, salads, filo pastries and pockets of Arab bread of the Middle East, as well as typical barbecues and whole roast lambs. In England an occasional hog roast will feed a whole community; Europe in late summer provides a constant feast of ripening grapes, figs and olives, with slices of garlicky, meaty salami in Italy; pizza bianca, hot from a village bakery; lasagne eaten from a cardboard dish sitting on Florentine steps, or a rough chunk of gritty parmesan with an apple, crunched between churches when sightseeing. In Spain, slices of jamón ibérico or manchego cheese with cubes of membrillo in the shade of a cork oak and in France the vast range of possible choices from a local market, *traiteur*, or even the stupendous supermarket where everything looks so much more desirable than at home.

In California the wealth of fruits and salads on show mean a picnic of free tastings before reaching the check out in a Napa Valley grocery store, or paying for a crowd-sized sandwich built at the deli counter of a Whole Foods supermarket in San Francisco. In Brazil a barbecue includes skewers of chicken hearts; quantities of meat top the bill for outdoor eating all over South America, supported by oceans of beans, bright salads and ubiquitous multicoloured corn on the cob. In South East Asia street eating starts at 5am in the markets of capital cities or small towns, with spicy dumplings, beef soup or chilli noodles, and Vietnamese street stalls sell instant picnics of fresh baguettes to eat with little pâtés wrapped in banana leaves.

Far to the North, whole salted herrings can be bought from hand carts in Dutch streets for eating on the spot; in Germany and Scandinavia, fat sausages with bread and a smear of strong mustard. In the Romanian Danube delta, a fisherman makes a *ciorba*, a fish soup of pike and catfish boiled outdoors over a fire, with vegetables and seasoning and in the Bulgarian mountain countryside where picnicking is popular, another soup, *kurban*, a meat stock coloured with peppers and tomatoes, is a traditional reminder of ancient animal sacrifices (Michael and Frances Field, *A Quintet of Cuisines*). Charcoal grilled corn on the cob is as much a staple street food in Eastern Europe as in South America or Africa where evening sales to hurrying pedestrians provide local women with a tiny income from surplus produce.

The nomadic peoples of Africa and Asia have nothing to learn about outdoor cooking and provisions, whether occasional feasts of meat and grains or the bare necessities for sustenance, a handful of dates in the desert; parched grain or *tsampa* in Tibet; the on the hoof meat larder of the Mongol herders, their long gone conquering hordes travelling ultra light, sustained mainly by drinking their horses' blood; the Masai and Nuer tribes, whose cattle provide their staples of milk and blood and only rarely meat. According to Reay Tannahill in *Food in History*, blood drinking or eating, has been common among pastoral peoples throughout history, the Arabs being particularly fond of a dish of mixed blood and camel hair and the Irish of a dish of blood boiled with milk, butter and herbs.

In the cities of North Africa and Turkey street sellers hawk their wares to peckish passersby and the streets are redolent of almond macaroons, oranges, frying doughnuts, sesame crusted bread and coffee. The Chinese are not obvious picnickers; one thinks instead of great formal dinners of perfectly balanced and presented courses, whether in the Forbidden City or the Great Hall of the People, but street stalls laden with soups, dumplings and orange coloured poultry offal offer scope for almost constant eating on the hoof. The focus of most Chinese festivals is on home and family and ancestral spirits need propitiation, their graves tended and their putative needs catered for; the Qingming Festival provides the best excuse for a family picnic in Chinese communities, when whole families and clans gather to sweep ancestors' graves and make offerings of wine and food to the dead followed by a grand graveside feast for the living.

The Victorians and Edwardians, at home and abroad may, aside from our own memories of picnics enjoyable or otherwise, be the inveterate picnickers at the centre of a picnic scene in our mind's eye although the use of the word picnic, in itself a Johnny-come-lately term for centuries of outdoor eating and packaged food, predates them by at least a century or so. Gilles Ménage's 1750 edition of the *Dictionnaire du Etymologique de la Langue Françoise* suggests that 'piquenique' may be of Spanish origin, first appearing in a French translation in 1664, although the Spanish do not use the word in any translation today. The *OED* dates the English translation to a letter from Lord Chesterfield in 1748 describing a social gathering and picnic thereafter became an expression for a shared outdoor meal to which participants all brought a dish, a definition with which *Larousse* concurs.

Introduction

Paying due deference to Victorian empire builders as indefatigable outdoor eaters wherever they were in the world, this book attempts, through the writings and memories of other feasters, fasters and travellers, to repeat tales that go beyond cold chicken and egg sandwiches in however many countries, to more unusual inventions, essentials and oddities of food and eating, carried, collected, prepared or eaten out of doors and away from formal kitchens, dining rooms and halls. In the end, it hardly matters what we call our outdoor feasts although there is no doubt, as Osbert Sitwell points out, that picnic is not a pretty word and there is no doubt that some of the descriptions of outdoor eating included in this book were, like war, no picnic at all.

First Picnics

If we begin only with the first use of the term picnic in whichever century or language it may first have been coined, we would lose an entire history of outdoor eating of one sort or another. A recent book on picnics opens with a group of 8th century monks seated on the ground to eat their meagre and carefully eked out supplies of cheese and salted horse head. They were wandering the famine stricken country with the miraculous relics of St Cuthbert after the sacking of Lindisfarne by the Vikings. It doesn't sound like much of a picnic (Jane Pettigrew quoting Reginald of Durham, *The Picnic*). Until the Romantic Movement transformed nature into art for those with the leisure and wealth to afford it, eating outdoors was more necessity than treat. Whether for conquerors and kings, religious or peasants, cooking and eating in the open were parts of everyday life, as they remain in parts of the world today. The concept of alfresco eating as entertainment is an 18th century invention, excepting perhaps at temples and churches on festivals and holy days, or when ancestral tombs were the sites of family gatherings and outdoor feasts that included both the living and the dead.

The best chronicled, if variably enumerated, mass outdoor meal of early modern history is well known. Whatever the size of the crowd, the actual numbers of loaves and fishes and whether or however they were miraculously multiplied, we assume that this was impromptu alfresco catering on a large scale.

From *Matthew, Chapter 15*:

> And Jesus saith unto them, How many loaves have ye? And
> they said, Seven, and a few little fishes.
> And he commanded the multitude to sit down on the ground.
> And he took the seven loaves and the fishes, and gave thanks,
> and brake them, and gave to his disciples, and the disciples to
> the multitude.
> And they did all eat, and were filled: and they took up of the
> broken meat that was left seven baskets full.
> And they that did eat were four thousand men, beside women
> and children.

Tinned kosher sardines from the Sea of Galilee can be bought on the
internet. Their ancestors are the most likely candidates for the 'two small
fishes' that, according to Matthew, Mark and John, with a loaves, barley
or otherwise, fed the four, five, or even twelve thousand, not including
unrecorded numbers of women and children. Morning caught sardines
are at their best grilled outdoors on some southern beach where their
smell is irresistibly inviting and a squeeze of lemon, bread and salt is all
that is needed for a perfect lunch. However fresh, they never taste quite
the same indoors in a restaurant.

Tinned sardines loom large in English food; in the nursery; on toast, as
a savoury in old-fashioned clubs and dining rooms; or as the easiest and
least large-boned of the endless smoked fish pâté starters of cut price 1970s
dinner parties. Elizabeth David wrote a typically well researched article,
Oules of Sardines, in 1962, that raised the profile of a humble little fish
into, at its best a product 'of some delicacy, a treat rather than an everyday

commodity'. In her day the French were, unsurprisingly, convinced of the pre-eminence of their sardines, fried in olive oil, over all others (*An Omelette and a Glass of Wine*). For French Foreign Legionnaires in Algeria in the 1960s, fighting on their stomachs meant lunches of bread, a tin of sardines and a raw onion eaten like an apple, washed down with a litre of rough wine.

Marika Hanbury Tenison, cookery editor of the *Sunday Telegraph* throughout the 1970s and wife of the explorer Robin, wrote in an article titled *First Catch Your Crocodile* that there were two 'basic requirements' for travelling with him, a tin of sardines and 'a large supply of celery salt, because jungle food is so tasteless...' The crocodile was 'really filthy' but the 'large red ants, fried to a crisp' were quite a successful addition to the essential sardines when dipped in the celery salt.

As children, sardine sandwiches were a teatime staple indoors and out, for tea on the lawn or the beach. In nursery days, while traditional battles waxed between nursery and kitchen, we ate what Nanny liked and by and large, excluding soft roes for breakfast, we liked what Nanny did. Her penchant for savoury over sweet resulted in shared picnics where our Marmite and lettuce, ham, or fishy sandwiches were occasionally unfavourably compared with our cousins' enviably sticky packages of sliced white bread filled with startlingly red jam. Our sardines were mashed into a rough paste with a little butter, not much less sophisticated than so-called sardine pâté and spread thinly on the strangely elongated rectangles of sliced white Scottish Mother's Pride. The delicious brown bread made in the kitchen by Mrs MacNeil in old Cow & Gate milk tins was not apparently considered suitable for sandwich making.

Brown bread in a milk tin

- 1 lb half plain, half wheaten flour
- 1 teaspoon baking soda
- 1 teaspoon Cream of Tartar
- 1 teaspoon salt
- 1 dessertspoon syrup
- Walnut-sized piece of butter

Mix altogether and add milk to make dropping consistency. Put into milk tin with lid and bake 1hr in moderate oven.

Mrs MacNeil cooked for us at our home on the Scottish West Coast island of Islay. I was only a few months old on my first visit and those early years of holidays and endless days with Nanny and my brother on a scrap of sand and rock, have blended into an undated memory of the gilded years of a peaceful and privileged childhood. I ate my first picnics on Islay and many more since, under the best or worst conditions. West Coast weather is not to be relied on; it can rain dismally for weeks on Islay or be transformed by days of bright sun, the hills and water shining in tweed colours making it the most beautiful place in the world.

As children we were dropped every morning at the beach with our buckets and spades and a good deal of Nanny's luggage. Mr MacNeil drove us down in the ancient, carefully nurtured LandRover, reappearing at lunch time with our picnic. If the rain came suddenly, gusting across the loch in grey sheets, we were reliant on him to drive back to the rescue, as we sheltered unsuccessfully in the lee of the rocks or paddled on happily, soaked to the skin, in the chilly rain-pocked shallows.

The best picnics were on Sundays when Mr and Mrs MacNeil took us on their day off expeditions to mysterious parts of the island and unfamiliar beaches. West Coast Scots, like their Irish near neighbours, have a taste for the macabre. Days out might include the graveyard and the ugly granite memorial, complete with ceramic photo plaque, to a recently dead baby, whose family was picked over like a chicken bone and whose image haunted me for weeks. The picnic itself was the high spot. Mrs MacNeil produced unexpected departures from our daily sandwiches and fruit; a flask of soup in addition to Nanny's usual tea; lamb rissoles or pieces of cold chicken; Mr MacNeil's tiny, matchless tomatoes, usually filched by us from the old conservatory attached to the house; an apple tart; buttered scones; or cakes of Mrs MacNeil's recent invention, the latest prize winners at the Womens' Institute, where she was the champion on an island full of good bakers.

When I was married in Wiltshire, Mrs MacNeil came south for the wedding and gave me as a wedding present a handwritten book of her recipes. None of them is very difficult or very exact. Their taste relies on good, fresh ingredients and, in the case of the apple tart, a lighter hand than I possess with pastry.

Creamy Carrot Soup

Coarsely grate 8oz carrots, 1 medium sized onion and a large potato; fry gently in 1oz of butter for 5 minutes, do not allow to brown.

Add ¾ pint of water and ¼ pint of milk; 1oz well-washed rice, a pinch of grated nutmeg, salt; bring to the boil, cover pan, lower heat and simmer very gently for ¾ - 1 hour.

Stir in 2 teaspoons lemon juice and 2-3 tablespoons fresh single cream. Reheat without boiling and sprinkle with chopped parsley before serving.

Apple Tart

For the short crust pastry: 6oz plain flour, 1¼ oz castor sugar, 3¼ oz block margarine (Stork)
Cream margarine and sugar in Kenwood mixer; add flour in tablespoonfuls and mix till well blended; knead on floured board till smooth and free from cracks.
Line pyrex plate with pastry (a tin plate will do, not a pie dish); dust lightly with cornflour to keep juice from soaking into pastry. Stew apples and when cold put onto pastry and cover with pastry lid. Prick all over with fork; make a slit in centre to let stead escape and decorate edges.
Bake ¾ - 1 hour in slow oven until pale brown.

It doesn't sound very exciting now, when children eat the same food as their parents and anticipate multi-national picnic menus that reflect both their well travelled palates and the shelves of the local supermarket. Unsophisticated country-bred sixties children lived lives much closer to the wartime childhoods of their parents' generation than to that of the last decades of the 20th century. In Islay the corn was still stacked in old-fashioned stooks to dry; our vegetables came from the garden; our butter, milk and cream, in large quantities, from the farm. Running around beaches in flowery pants and hateful itchy fairisle jerseys, the height of our cosmopolitan ambition was reached with German cocktail sausages eaten straight from their little jars of brine.

We were sent to Scotland from our home in the South of England at the beginning of the summer holidays. Oh the excitement of the night train from Euston to Glasgow Central station and breakfast in the Central Hotel, starting with tomato juice, then porridge, eggs, kippers, toast and tea. On another train to the port of Gouroch, we caught our first delicious smell of the sea, then two successive ferries to Islay, with lunch in the white-clothed dining room on the second. Nanny suffered from travel sickness that necessitated the small and interesting medicinal flask of brandy in her handbag.

up the storm-clouds over the Ben behind you. A situation of this sort subdues even a Scotch keeper's omnivorous capacity for remnants, and the dogs get a larger share than usual of the crumbs which fall from their master's table. Yet the lunch on the moor is the lunch of the highest possibilities, which only require for their realisation a fine day. A lunch amid the purple heather, with a cloudless sky overhead, and just a ruffle of mountain breeze to tone down the effect of the blazing sun, which enables you to appreciate the cool waters of the burn brattling down the hillside into the blue loch below – such a lunch knows no rival in this present vale of tears.'

The advent of the disposable barbecue has added to the variety of easy picnic food for Scottish family picnics and improved the lot of the fed up holiday cook. Whereas a proper barbecue needs coaxing to light and careful nurturing to turn the flames to glowing charcoal, these tin foil trays of charcoal can be lit in a force 8 gale and will cook a few sausages in minutes; real barbecues need real cleaning too. Raw meat can be chucked into a bag and the cook abnegate all further responsibility to those with a fire fetish. The meat for fast heating and cooking throwaways benefits from advance dousing with soy or Worcestershire sauce, pepper and garlic salt, although local Scottish lamb and fillet steaks melt like butter and are consumed in appalling quantities by the usual army of enormous, immensely hungry teenage boys.

Gifts of sides of smoked salmon or gravadlax from the Loch Fyne Smokery are welcome additions to the Scottish holiday larder and picnic. Digby Anderson, the *Spectator*'s Imperative Cook gives clear instructions, with diagrams, for the construction of a home smoker, a proper thing with a chamber and a chimney (*Imperative Food*). It all sounds a bit like hard work but making Gravadlax is easy as pie, cheap as chips and successful with salmon of most inferior provenance. Two sides sandwiched together under layers of dill, sugar and salt and weighted at the bottom of the fridge for a week will be good enough for the fussiest foodie. There is no great magic or skill required to whisk up mustard and dill sauce to go with it and dried dill works just fine. In Islay, a little way offshore, there is a small uninhabited island, reached by boat on calmer days, with the perfect flat coffin-shaped stone just above the beach, for carving cured sides of fish while barbecues are lit on the pebbles below.

Tinned sardines have disappeared from recent picnics in the face of such riches. Lately there have been oysters too, from an island farm using its location on the shores of a sea loch to diversify into oyster production. The oyster beds provide the nuttiest, freshest taste of the sea, and with an oyster knife, Tabasco and a lemon, an instant picnic in the adjacent dunes. The opposite shore of the loch is the place for huge lunch time gatherings of friends and extended family, 40 or more cousins and kinsmen, with ill-assorted packs of dogs, the best bred spaniels and the most mistakenly born mongrels in every size and shape. An excess of lobsters from the local lobster man means the remains of dinner as lobster mayonnaise, another luxury addition to ham or barbecued sausages of which Lady Jekyll would have approved. Lobster is unfortunately much to the taste of the 'dorgies', two badly mannered, low-slung and hairy sisters with royal connections and mixed ancestry for whom a plastic box with an ill-fitting lid is no obstacle to joint endeavour and intense greed.

Enough alcohol is essential to the multi-generational beach picnic, oiling old and arthritic appreciation of the young, ravenous and incredibly loud and encouraging healing post-prandial sleep for all ages. My husband's Bloody Mary recipe is straight from the Dean Martin school of cocktail making – for choice his vodka is lightly coloured with tomato juice. For more general use, he considers himself, after years of experimentation, to have the perfect formula, which is made and drunk in industrial quantities.

Equipment-Fanatics who use cologne impregnated ones hoarded from their air-flights to Tenerife. Car rugs are good for wiping hands on.

Take plenty of cold roast birds; pheasants, partridges, chickens, a few teal or widgeon. But first perhaps some fish pâté, some turbot steaks with mayonnaise or artichoke hearts in oil. There should always be potatoes in their jackets. They are taken out of the oven just before departure and wrapped in old towels with some bottles of claret and put in the warmest place. By lunchtime they won't be very warm but the claret will be better than it would have been.'

The authors of *Cook Away* would approve a 'Chaps' picnic that 'necessitates considerable preparation ahead of time'. Their strictures for their five categories of successful alfresco eating exclude the claret but are clear on the importance of a good alcohol supply, especially in the camper van: 'Lack of space prevents much of a wine cellar but even the smallest of these temporary homes should have on hand Scotch, Bourbon or rye whisky, brandy and sherry for medicinal and culinary reasons if no other. Many will want to augment this minimum supply with gin, vermouth, both French and Italian, Angostura bitters and rum'. A fairly extensive driving drinks cupboard one would think, providing the makings of some useful medicinal cocktails; Manhattans; old-fashions mint juleps; and any number of Martinis.

Martini Cocktail No.1

3 parts gin

1 part combined ½ French vermouth/
½ Italian vermouth

Place in a shaker with ice. Stir well, don't
shake. An olive may be placed in each glass

Boating Feasts and Follies

'It is not the first object of your work to keep down expenditure, but it is your first duty to see a table of superior quality maintained on board your ship, and your passengers thoroughly well satisfied. It has seldom happened that a really good table was not an economical one, compared to one badly managed, but you must clearly understand that what we now instruct you to secure is first an excellent table, and secondly to combine your efforts in that direction with due economy; and it is the wish of the Directors that you should continually seek to improve the table arrangements on board your ship.'

(Memorandum for the Guidance of Pursers and Stewards-in-Charge on Victualling and Management, 1908, P & O Company.)
(Theodore Fitzgibbon, *The Pleasures of the Table*)

Gerald Durrell's descriptions of their life in pre World War II Corfu have fixed his idiosyncratic family, mother cooking endlessly for eccentric guests at its centre, in the imaginations of generations of his readers, and gilded Prospero's island with added magic. The story of Mother's birthday party from *Fillets of Plaice* begins with the accident-prone loading of the family's massive and far from portable ice box onto a *benzina* for a boat picnic on a grand scale and gives us one of the most memorable pictures of the family, their friends and their food.

'Then, eventually we reached the extraordinary brown and eroded coast between Albania and Corfu which spread on into Greece, and as we drew closer and closer to the coast we passed towering pinnacles of rock like the carunculated melted remains of a million multicoloured candles. Eventually, as night was falling, we discovered a bay that looked as though it had been bitten out of the hard rock by some gigantic sea monster. It was a perfect half moon, and here we thought we would make landfall. The sand was white, the cliffs tall and somehow protective, and so gently the benzina was brought in, the anchor was thrown over the side, and we came to a halt. This was the moment when the ice-box came into its own. Out of it Mother and Spiro unpacked an incredible assortment of foodstuffs: legs of lamb stuffed with garlic, lobsters, and various extraordinary things that Mother had made which she called curry puffs. Some of them were in fact curry puffs but others were stuffed with different delicacies. And so we lay around on the deck and gorged ourselves.

In the forequarters of the boat we had a great pile of watermelons that looked like an array of pudgy footballs, green with whitish stripes on them. Periodically, one of these would be popped into the ice-box and then brought out so that we could cut it open. The pink and beautiful inside was as crisp as any ice-cream that you could ever wish for.'

For Mother's birthday lunch the following day the party ate freshly caught *kefalia*, flathead mullet grilled over charcoal and, later, dinner of 'octopus and tiny cuttlefish that had been ensconced in the ice-box, followed by cold chicken and fruit'. The next day's disaster, when the *benzina* failed to start and supplies ran low, culminated in salvation by the redoubtable master of all work, Spiro. He appeared with the sunset in the bows of a fishing boat 'like a massive bulldog', with 'a whole roasted sheep on a spit and beside it a great basket containing all the fruits of the season'.

Vivid descriptions of a long gone Corfu evoke memories of other picnics carried by boat to hidden harbours on sunny pine-scented islands. On

Turtle Steaks Marchand de Vin (Gourmet Cookbook)

Rub 6 individual turtle steaks with a damp cloth dipped in a little vinegar. Dip each steak into seasoned flour, in beaten egg, and finally in sieved bread crumbs. Heat 1.4 cup butter and stir in 1 tablespoon finely chopped shallots. Cook the steaks in this to a delicate brown on both sides. Pour over the browned steaks 1 cup Bordeaux and season with salt, pepper, and a dash of nutmeg. Cover the pan and simmer gently for 15 to 20 minutes. Dress the steaks on a hot platter and keep hot.

Reduce the sauce in the pan over a hot flame to almost nothing. Stir in ¼ cup rich beef stock, ½ cup sherry, and 1 cup thinly sliced mushrooms, cooked in a little butter. Taste for seasoning. Pour a little of the sauce over each steak and serve the rest in a sauceboat. Garnish with water cress.

Clear Mock Turtle Soup (Potage de Tortue, Fausse, Clair.)

½ a calf's head, 5 quarts of clear Second Stock (or water), 2 onions, 2 carrots, 1 turnip, a strip of celery, bouquet-garni (parsley, basil, marjoram, thyme, bay-leaf). 12 peppercorns, 4 cloves, 2 blades of mace, 2 glasses of sherry, 1 tablespoon of lemon-juice, ½ a lb of lean beef, ½ a lb of lean veal, the whites and shells of 2 eggs, salt.

Soak the head 24 hours in salt and water, changing it frequently. Then bone the head (the brains and tongue may be used for some other purpose), tie the meant in a thin cloth and break the bones into small pieces; put them into a stewpan, cover with cold water, add a tablespoonful of salt, let it boil up, strain, and was the head in cold water. Return the meat and bones to the stewpan, put in the stock and a dessertspoonful of salt, boil up, and skim well. Now add the prepared vegetables, herbs, peppercorns, cloves and mace, and when boiling, remove the scum, put on the cover and cook slowly for about 3 hours according to the size of the head. Strain, put the meat aside, and when the stock is cold remove the fat, and clarify with the coarsely chopped beef and veal and whites of eggs. Return to the saucepan, with the sherry, the lemon-juice and a little of the meat of the head, cut into small pieces. Add necessary seasoning, boil up and serve.

(Mrs Beeton's *Household Management*)

On Christmas Day 1827, the Duke was on board the *Anna Eliza* in port at Messina in Sicily. He had been unwell but was still keen that the festival should be celebrated in proper style.

> 'My ship's company had a plentiful hot dinner served to them, and my warrant-officers had another on the quarter-deck. My servants had a third. An allowance of beer was given them, as well as wine. In the evening I got two fiddles and a harp on board; a quart of warm punch per man was served out to the whole ship's company; dancing began and continued all evening. The men enjoyed themselves beyond measure'.

> (Roberts and Morgan-Grenville, *No Ordinary Tourist*)

George Cheyne took a dim view of punch in his *Essay of Health and Long Life* in 1745, but punches and similar spirituous mixtures in one form or another flow through records of food and drink since the earliest times and particularly those of sailors.

'Next to Drams, no Liquor deserves more to be stigmatised and banished the repasts of the tender, valetudinary, and studious, than Punch. 'Tis a composition of such Parts, as not one of them is salutary or kindly to such constitutions, except the pure element, in it. The principal ingredient is Ru, Arrack, Brandy, or Malt Spirits ... The other principal part of the composition is the juice of oranges and lemons. And if we consider, that a lemon or orange could never be transported half seas over to us, without rotting or spoiling, if gathered when wholly ripe, we should have no great opinion of their juices.'

Mrs Beeton's Hot Punch (1839)

- 1/2 pint of rum
- 1/2 pint of brandy
- 1/4 lb. of sugar
- 1 large lemon
- 1/2 teaspoonful of nutmeg
- 1 pint of boiling water.

Mode. Rub the sugar over the lemon until it has absorbed all the yellow part of the skin, then put the sugar into a punchbowl; add the lemon-juice (free from pips), and mix these two ingredients well together. Pour over them the boiling water, stir well together, add the rum, brandy, and nutmeg; mix thoroughly, and the punch will be ready to serve. It is very important in making good punch that all the ingredients are thoroughly incorporated; and, to insure success, the processes of mixing must be diligently attended to.

Sufficient. Allow a quart for 4 persons; but this information must be taken cum grano salis; for the capacities of persons for this kind of beverage are generally supposed to vary considerably.

The young artist Sidney Parkinson, accompanied Joseph Banks, the naturalist and explorer, on Captain Cook's 1768 voyage to the South Pacific. Parkinson, before himself succumbing to dysentery, left a remarkable illustrated journal that provides some curious insights into a medicinally experimental-sounding ship's diet in which various turtles were some of the least bizarre components. By this time the means of avoiding the sailors' curse of scurvy were fairly well understood although there is a view that Cook, with his less reported belief in the anti-scorbutic efficacy of malt over fresh citrus fruit, was not as responsible for its decline as his legend would have it. Others like the Scottish doctor, James Lind, tested a variety of remedies including 'cyder', 'elixir of vitriol'* and 'a course of seawater', before confirming that 'the most sudden and visible good effects were perceived from the use of the oranges and lemons; one of those who had taken them being at the end of six days fit for duty.'

> Take of Sulphuric Acid three troy ounces;
> Fluid Extract of Orange Peel, one fluid ounce;
> Red Rose Leaves, two drachms;
> Boiling Water, one fluid ounce;
> Alcohol, a sufficient quantity.

> Add the acid gradually to half a pint of alcohol, and pour the boiling water upon the rose leaves; When both liquids have become cool, unite them, add the fluid extract and sufficient alcohol to make up the measure of eighteen fluid ounces. Mix thoroughly and filter.

> Elixir of vitriol, thus prepared, has a pleasant aromatic odor and flavour, and the beautiful red color of the rose leaves, heightened by the presence of the acid. It is miscible with water without turbidity, and a specimen, after long keeping, has deposited but a trace of sediment.

Parkinson's descriptions include some foods that may have been a better antidote against scurvy than others; fresh meat must certainly have been an improvement over salted and the explorers were ready and willing to try whatever came their way.

---

*. Elixir of Vitriol otherwise known as Aromatic Sulphuric Acid sounds a pretty refreshment in this version from *The American Journal of Pharmacy* of 1871.

Whilst those well-travelled 'lucent syrops' and 'soother' jellies might owe their existence to poetic fancy, they gleam on in the mind's eye, and, with the jewel-like crystallised fruits, arranged for their beauty in the moonlight, encourage further flights of fantasy. The dates, fat and bursting, elegantly stuffed with nuts or almond paste; the metaphorical manna, who knows? A metaphor for bread? A sweet saffron coloured brioche perhaps? And more; gilded diamonds of marchpane, flavoured with rose water; orange lokum; sherbet to drink, or a smooth milk punch spiked with spirit; silver baskets of roasted pistachios; and tiny savoury pastries, barely a mouthful, flavoured with mint and coriander.

Of course none of it got eaten, unless by palsied old Angela or the mice, as Porphyro and his lover, Madeline, stole silently away from the castle into the freezing January night, while her father, Porphyro's sworn enemy, feasted in the hall with his blood-thirsty kinsmen.

> *And they are gone: ay, ages long ago*
> *These lovers fled away into the storm.*
> *That night the Baron dreamt of many a woe,*
> *And all his warrior-guests, with shade and form*
> *Of witch, and demon, and large coffin-worm,*
> *Were long be-nightmar'd. Angela the old*
> *Died palsy-twitch'd, with meagre face deform;*
> *The Beadsman after thousand aves told,*
> *For aye unsought for slept among his ashes cold.*

Milk Punch (The Practical Housewife, Anon, 1860)

Peel the yellow zest from 3 lemons and place in a large bowl. Squeeze the lemons and pour the juice through a sieve onto the zest. Stir in 200 grams of granulated sugar, 500ml of water and 375ml of rum. Heat 123ml of whole milk to boiling point, pour over other ingredients, cover bowl and leave in a cool place for 24 hours. Line a sieve with two or three layers of butter muslin, place over a jug, and filter punch through the muslin, then pour into a clean bottle. Cork and keep in a cool place until required. Serve cold, in glasses or by ladling from a punch bowl.

Sir Kenelm Digby is best known for his 17th century cookbook *The Closet of the Eminently Learned Sir Kenelme Digbie Opened*. He was an eccentric intellectual of wide interests and something of a romantic figure, whether beloved, according to his own account, of Marie de Medici, or just much loved by the women he served who included Queen Henrietta Maria. His recipes are full of the exotic romance of Keats's imagined picnic and these strengthening tablets of properly aphrodisiac ingredients, pearls, musk and ambergris, unfortunately beyond the scope of most modern cooks.

Pleasant Cordial Tablets,
which are very comforting, and strengthen nature much

Take four ounces of blanched Almonds; of Pine kernels, and of Pistachios, ana, four Ounces. Erin-go-roots, Candid-Limon peels, ana, three Ounces, Candid Orange peels two Ounces, Candid Citron-peels four Ounces, of powder of white Amber, as much as will lie upon a shilling; and as much of the powder of pearl, 20 grains of Ambergreece, three grains of Musk, a book of leaf gold, Cloves and Mace, of each as much as will lie upon a three pence; cut all these as small as possible you can. Then take a pound of Sugar, and half a pint of water, boil it to a candy-height, then put in the Ambergreece and Musk, with three or four spoonfulls of Orange flower water. Then put in all the other things and stir them well together, and cast them upon plates, and set them to dry: when both sides are dry, take Orange-flower-water and Sugar, and Ice them.

My Lord of Denbigh's Almond March-Pane

Blanch Nut-Kernels from the Husks in the best manner you can. Then put them with a due proportion of Sugar, and a little Orange-flower, or Rose-water. When it is in a fitting uniform paste, make it into round Cakes, about the bigness of your hand, or a little larger, and about a finger thick; and lay every one upon a fine paper cut fit to it; which lay upon a table. You must have a pan like a tourtiere, made to contain coals on the top, that is flat, with edges round about to hold in the coals, which set over the Cakes, with fire upon it. Let this remain upon the Cakes, till you conceive, it hath dryed them sufficiently for once; which may be within a quarter of an hour; but you take it off two or three times in that time, to see you scorch not the outside, but only dry it a little. Then remove it to others, that lye by them; and pull the Papers from the first, and turn them upon new Papers. When the others are dryed enough, remove the pan back to the first, to dry their other side: which being enough, remove it back to the second, that by this time are turned, and laid upon new Papers. Repeat this turning the Cakes, and changing the Pan, till they are sufficiently dry: which you must not do all at once, least you scorch them: and though the outside be dry, the inside must be very moist and tender. Then you must Ice them thus: Make a thick pap with Orange flower or Rose-water, and purest white Sugar: a little of the whites of Eggs, not above half a spoonful of that Oyl of Eggs, to a Porrenger full of thick Pap, beaten exceeding well with it, and a little juyce of Limons. Lay this smooth upon the Cakes with a Knife, and smoothen it with a feather. Then set the pan over them to dry them. Which being if there be any unevenness, or cracks or discolouring, lay on a little more of that Mortar, and dry it as before. Repeat this, till it be as clear, and smooth, and white, as you would have it. Then turn the other sides, and do the like to them. You must take care, not to scorch them: for then they would look yellow or red, and they must be pure, white and smooth like Silver between polished and matte, or like a looking Glass. This Coat preserves the substance of the Cakes within, the longer moist. You may beat dissolved Amber, or Essence of Cinnamon, with them.

Food for Lovers, a *1977* book with recipes by Katie Stewart and Ken Lo, is disappointingly short on fantastic dishes although the introduction discusses the demerits of various purported aphrodisiacs, many of which, like Spanish Fly or cantharides can be lethal.[*] The book suggests that a cucumber salad should be avoided at your romantic picnic; according to the Elizabethan physician and traveller Andrew Boorde, it 'restrayneth veneryousnes, or lassyuyousnes, or luxuryousnes'. He may have known what he was talking about since he was eventually convicted of keeping loose women in his lodgings at Winchester, and, in other stipulations on the importance of cleanliness in the house and especially the kitchen, was

---

[*]. Spanish Fly was finally banned from sale in the spice markets of Morocco only in the 1990s and is still advertised for sale on the internet. Its deadly effects were demonstrated when the Marquis de Sade poisoned two prostitutes with copiously laced aniseed sweets, three others, who perhaps did not like aniseed, survived. As recently as 1954, in London, Arthur Ford gave doctored coconut bonbons to an office colleague with whom he was infatuated and managed to poison both her and a friend who ate them too. Those looking for a moral might suggest that eating really disgusting sweets is bad for the health as the drug appears not to have a taste that needs powerful disguise. Alan Davidson provides a more amusing anecdote from Moroccan research on the use of the aphrodisiac. He 'dissolved into laughter and, between laughs, related how his wife had once added some to a pan of spaghetti which she was boiling. When she came to serve this, she found that every single strand of spaghetti was standing bolt upright in the pan.' (Alan Davidson, *Oxford Companion*)

well ahead of his time. The authors of *Food for Lovers* believe that picnics have always been a favourite pursuit of the amorous but their lovers' picnics, divided into those suitable for rich, poor, hurried, or not, sound a great deal more depressing than their indoor meals. It is hard to imagine that 'Pickled or Soused Herrings with Rice Salad', beer or cider and fresh plums would encourage the poverty stricken to amatory adventures; or that salami or pizza for the hurried lover, in 'your basket with a pretty cloth', would produce summits of passion; although 'luscious peaches' sound quite nice. The lover with time to spare can manufacture 'chicken balls' and a 'pineapple dessert' for a picnic which sounds to me like the bitter end.

Edward Lear captures a far more romantic picnic, a honeymoon too.

The Owl and the Pussycat
The Owl and the Pussycat went to sea
In a beautiful pea-green boat,
They took some honey, and plenty of money,
Wrapped up in a five pound note.
The Owl looked up to the stars above,
And sang to a small guitar,
"O lovely Pussy! O Pussy, my love,
What a beautiful Pussy you are, you are, you are,
What a beautiful Pussy you are."
Pussy said to the Owl "You elegant fowl,
How charmingly sweet you sing.
O let us be married, too long we have tarried;
But what shall we do for a ring?"
They sailed away for a year and a day,
To the land where the Bong-tree grows,
And there in a wood a Piggy-wig stood
With a ring at the end of his nose, his nose, his nose,
With a ring at the end of his nose.
"Dear Pig, are you willing to sell for one shilling your ring?"
Said the Piggy, "I will"
So they took it away, and were married next day

By the Turkey who lives on the hill.
They dined on mince, and slices of quince,
Which they ate with a runcible spoon.
And hand in hand, on the edge of the sand
They danced by the light of the moon, the moon, the moon,
They danced by the light of the moon.

While the mince sounds worthy but hardly exciting, there are recipes for quince and meat stews or quince with meat stuffing in Iranian cuisine and the quince itself has long been considered a fruit of love. The ancient Greeks held the quince sacred to Aphrodite, the goddess of love to whom Paris gave the golden apple of the Hesperides. Golden apples were synonymous with quinces, appearing also in Norse mythology as the food of immortality of the gods and, most probably, as the 'apples' of the *Song Of Solomon.* There are innumerable recipes for quince jellies, preserves and tarts in Middle Eastern and older English cookbooks and the honeymooners knew what they were doing with their supply of honey. Soyer tells us the quince possesses 'the most beneficial qualities' and 'marvellous virtues.'

'This fruit, so much extolled, was preserved by placing it with its branches and leaves in a vessel, afterwards filled with honey or sweet wine'. (Alexis Soyer, *Food, Cookery and Dining in Ancient Times*)

> 'In the best stories, the standard bill of fare is, I believe, cold venison pie, a good red wine, a couple of apples and some nuts...'
> 'Venison pie? It is one of the great alfresco delicacies. I have, ever since I put away childish things, made a firm rule: I will eat well prepared indoor things outdoors, and suitably delicious outdoor food, indoors; I will not, however, put myself in the double jeopardy of eating outdoor food outdoors. If I'm to suffer ants, spiders, dirt on my hands, and stones under my backside, I must have a touch of civilisation to take the curse off it. I'm not so degenerate as to insist on the wicker basket

and the red-and-white-checkered cloth – just degenerate enough to be convinced that everything tastes better if you have them.

At any rate venison is the archetypal pie that everything else is as easy as. You take a pie plate large enough to accommodate the remainder of your venison stew (which you have made with a good red-wine marinade plus some onions and mushrooms – but without potatoes, dumplings, carrots, parsnips or rutabagas). Next you line the plate with plain pastry, put in the stew, add a top crust, crimp the edge, cut a round hole in the centre, and bake till the pastry is nicely browned. You then cool it in the tin, wrap it in foil, and throw it in your knapsack. With a Cabernet, if you can afford it – or a four liter jug of red plonk, if you can carry it – there is no sickness that destroyeth in the noonday against which you will not have at least a fighting chance. *In vino veritas. Prosit!'*

Cornish Pasty 1922, St Ives

Flour ½ lb; lard or dripping 3oz; a pinch of salt; water to make a fine dough about 1gill (2½ liquid ounces). Uncooked beef steak ½lb; uncooked calf's liver ¼lb; uncooked potatoes 2; onion 1 large one; turnip 1 medium sized one; carrot 1 large or 2 small ones. Pepper and salt.

To bake 1 hour; at first in a good oven to raise the pastry and then in a very moderate oven to cook the meat and vegetables.

Roll out the dough fairly thin, cut in squares.

Chop the steak and liver finely, mix together and season.

Peel or scrape and slice the potato, onion, turnip and carrot. Mix and season the vegetables.

Put a layer of vegetables on half of each square of pastry and some of the chopped meat on top.

Brush the edges of the pastry with white of egg, fold the plain half over the meat and pinch the edge well together.

Bake as above.

N.B. – It is important to close the edges neatly and closely, so that no steam escapes, and to use uncooked meat and vegetables. The contents cook in their own juices, so after the first few minutes require a very moderate oven. The above amounts make 2 large or 3 medium- sized pasties.

(Good Things in England)

Atwood Clark's *Country Mix – Reminiscences of Rural Life and Sport in 19th Century England* draws on memories of South West England, in particular the Wiltshire villages, the downs and the rivers, close to where I live. The impenetrable Wiltshire accent he transcribes to give such character to some of his stories and best read aloud for understanding, only lives on now in the vocal shades and inflections of the most elderly speakers.

> 'Elevenses'. Blessed word! The workers have been thinking of it for an hour or more, and it was the exception rather than the rule for them to swallow a draught of anything liquid until the sun was high. If you did you would be thirsty all day... there is a rattle of wheels from the farm gig, driven by the farmer's

wife, with a brace of 'bustious' boys of walking age perched beside her. With them are the half of a forty-pound cheese, a large 'batch' of bread, and an eighteen-gallon cask of home-brewed beer.

As each mower 'cuts out' he sets the blade of his scythe forward for safety into the uncut grass... Then wiping his forehead, and his mind concentrating on one great central thought, he makes for the gateway. Arrived, he notes a dissolving cluster of women who are bearing full jars and baskets from the gig. There is the moisture he craves and a cask with a tap already inserted. Beer! His wife meets him and hands an uncorked jar. He nods briefly, draws his hand across sticky, clammy lips, and lifts the familiar vessel... The old gods must have had attractive temporal joys to offer mortals if they had better things to give than the all-absorbing ecstasy of that draught.

There is a laugh from some young ones when one of the older men, who in passing the gig halted for a moment to view the cheese, which is being cut into mighty chunks by the farm mistress, and then lowered his head and peered. 'Fine cheese thickee, missis. Zee wur mousies's bin.' The laugh from the others is followed by affirmative murmurs, for every countryman knows that if there is a great pile of cheeses in the storage loft and a rare mouse finds its way to them and finally, after inspection, nibbles one, the cheese selected for the honour is surely the finest of them all. The common mouse is truly the best judge of good cheese in the world.

Summer work and rewards must have seemed another country as winter took it's freezing hold, although the following story from the lambing season of around 1810 obviously gave much amusement to its aged teller, in retrospect.

As things turned out they were weather-bound for four days before being able to cross three snowdrifted miles to the homestead.

'Thur wur nout ter do so us taarked and sumtime sung ims. But Zeb ee ad a vice wuss nor anny owd craw. Twur drefful ter ear un, an'our bellies wor emptier nor anny drum. Zeb ee ad korns an gat cauld veet as well, so ee taaked orf 'is bootses an' wropt is veet en a bit of ould zack. Wied bin boorwin'into thick straw (an troid ter ate un, us wor that thrawed) vor vour nights. On the laarst Zeb ee groned an snoared turble. Oi cudn't slape a winksie; oi wur that craavin' vor vittals.

Moi 'and cum gainst wun ov Zeb's bootses an oi thort twud be bettern nor nout, so oi toikes moi knoife an cuts orf most ov topsoide on im. Oi sloices thickee inter teeny bitses an chews thickee arl noight vore oi gits un daown. Thort ter ate the soal on un vore morning, but shipherd ee rousts up an' as a moind ter taaka looksee outside. Then er vound thick bit ov boot as oi'd lef un. Proper stark chap wor Zeb, an' vore oi cud move ee ad oi vast. Eer eld oi toight an' ad orf wum ov moi bootses. The ee cut orf top loike oi ad dun ter issen an chewd us as ef a loiked un. All toime ee luked main sour at oi an' simmed 'mazed wi honger soides. Oi wuz yung an tender those days an oi gits praaper veared, twuz oi. So oi thort twuz toime ter say as us ad better kill owd Blossom vor ter ate. Laks! Then oi thort ee was gwine ter murder oi roight smart; but ee onny made a drefful vaice an laned across oi an' gritted 'is toothen and maaked a nise loike a girt dog an' cussed oi. The er sed: "Oi'll zee tis theesen wot es ate vore oid vace maister wi bits o' Blossom insoide oi." Ee luked loike Bellsbub, oi tell ee.'

(Atwood Clark, *Country Mix*)

As to the river of the *Reminiscences*, it is the Kennet, also part of my fishing memories, although as much for summer picnic teas as great catches. Comfortably warm afternoons with older, more expert, fishing friends, free with teaching advice as to flies, casts, strategy; with quicker eyes for a trout, seen too late by me as he flicks his tail, speeding towards invisibility. Teas were simple enough, freshly made flaky little sausage rolls, cakes by Mr Kipling, whichever iced slice the current favourite of our host and delicious bottled lemonade, one of those with pretensions to home-made style. The point was as much the break as the food, an excuse for lying idle, horizontal, dozy, under the summer sky in the warm hay-smelling grass, before dragging ourselves up again to the business in hand; as often catching the bank; once as an unfortunate bet, an unsuspecting water rat; or a 'filthy' grayling; or as our target, the shy shining brown trout.

Views on the grayling do differ; Alfred E. T. Watson points out that 'Grayling are not bad eating, if properly cooked – that is, split open and grilled'. Izaak Walton was impressed more by their medicinal properties:

> 'The fat of an Umber or Grayling, being set, with a little honey,
> a day or two in the sun, in a little glass, is very excellent against
> redness or swarthiness, or anything that breeds in the eyes.'
> (Izaak Walton, *The Compleat Angler*)

Truth be told few fish straight from the river taste too bad with skin charred instantly on a throwaway barbecue, if such things are allowed, and a dash of salt and lemon. With the introduction into rivers of fat bred rainbow and brown trout, the delicate and delicious wild brown is ever rarer. Far and few in the Kennet are the wild four and five pounders of the late 19th century when Atwood Clark wrote of 'Kennet Monsters' that 'cut as pink as any sea-trout... and tasted better'.

'Anglers Roast Trout

Scour, wash, open and clean the fish as usual; then cut off their heads, score them lightly, and pepper and salt them inside and out; cut one or more branches (sweet birch is best), and stick the fish upon the twigs, running the twig along the upper side of the back-bone, hold the branch before the fire; by watching the inside of the fish it is easy to see when they are done.'

(The Unrivalled Cook and Housekeepers Guide, Mrs Washington)

'What say you, scholar, to the providence of an old angler? Does not this meat taste well? And was not this place well chosen to eat it? For this sycamore-tree will shade us from the sun's heat.'
(The Compleat Angler)

Eiffel Tower Lemonade made from concentrated crystals is the picnic beverage, precursor to today's boutique mixes, that has stuck most in the memories of children of the late 19th and early 20th century, in company with sandwiches and little iced cakes sprinkled with hundreds and thousands.

'When I was a child, almost 60 years ago, Swindon had its Trip week. All who worked 'inside' were transported to seaside destinations by special Trip trains. The longest journeys to Penzance and St Ives left late in the evening and arrived before breakfast. The highlight of the journey was food, sandwiches, tea in a Thermos for the grown ups and lemonade made with Eiffel Tower crystals for the children (no buffet cars on Trip trains) – and delight of delight, Butter Puffs and triangular cream cheeses.' *(Wiltshire, Within Living Memory)*

Eiffel Tower advertisements were evocative and persuasive:

'Partly prepared in sunny Sicily from ripe, fragrant, luscious Messina Lemons, the choicest Lemons the world produces.
Scores of peasants gather the Lemons from the trees, they are then taken direct from the Lemon Orchards into the Factory to commence their transformation into 'Eiffel Tower' Concentrated Lemonade. In this way thousands and thousands of bushels of the Finest Lemons are used every year. It is by this careful selection of the finest fruit only that the delicious flavor of 'Eiffel Tower' Lemonade is obtained.
This delicious beverage is pre-eminently the best drink for children, because of its health-giving properties.'

And:

> 'As supplied to the House of Commons'

> As it turned out, however delicious and however many MPs Eiffel Tower refreshed, it barely contained lemon at all, let alone the 38,000,000 per year claimed by the the makers of the 'Concoction', against whom a judgment was upheld in 1901. On analysis it had been found instead to contain 'about 40 per cent. of tartaric acid, 44 per cent. of cane sugar, 5 per cent. of oil of lemon and coloring matter, and 2 per cent. of water.' Justice O'Brien, for the court, decreed that 'There can be no possible escape from the conclusion that the article was held out to the public as made from lemon juice and that the beverage formed by its admixture with water was lemonade. As neither representation was true and the product was but an imitation or simulation of lemonade, the verdict is amply sustained.' (*New York Times*, 2nd May 1901)

The concentrated drink that added to the problems of the *Three Men in a Boat* sounds very much like Eiffel Tower:

> 'I reminded him that there was concentrated lemonade in the hamper, and a gallon-jar of water in the nose of the boat, and that the two only wanted mixing to make a cool and refreshing beverage.

> Then he flew off about lemonade, and "such-like Sunday-school slops", as he termed them, ginger-beer, raspberry syrup, &c., &c. He said they all produced dyspepsia, and ruined body and soul alike, and were the cause of half the crime in England.'

The Idris soft drinks factory was another source of ready-made lemonade and a ginger beer that still bears the Idris name although now manufactured by Britvic. The Idris factory was the site of a landmark strike in 1911 by the women workers in support of their demands for better conditions. They worked 'ankle deep in poorly drained water', and drank tea in their break that was 'boiled from the same water that had already been used to slop down the floor'. They walked out of the factory singing:

Fisher's example only in more liquid forms of refreshment. The most encouraging part of her lunch was clearly the large slug of bourbon from her flask, slightly diluted with airline water. Alcohol so often puts a rosier glow on things.

As it turned out the gastronomic efforts of this particular airline were not yet exhausted. Shortly before landing, and, fortified with another slug from her flask, Fisher was presented with a beribboned cellophane box full of fruit and enclosing a paper slip that said: 'You may eat this with carefree abandon, for it has been washed and scrubbed and rub-a-dub-dubbed.'

Anthony Trollope's 1869 description of the railway sandwich in *He Knew He Was Right* leads the reader to awareness that contemporary railway catering has returned to its roots: 'the real disgrace of England is the railway sandwich, that whited sepulchre, fair enough outside, but so meagre, poor, and spiritless within, such a thing of shreds and parings, with a dab of food'.

When we were young, things were different or seemed so. Our winter day trips by train to London from Wiltshire meant easing the old-fashioned stiffness of Rowes tweed coats with velvet collars and velvet hats with dining car silver service breakfasts where white coated waiters offered porridge or cereal, followed by bacon, mushrooms, eggs and toast and marmalade. Toasted tea cakes on the 4.30 from Paddington return were accompanied by those little pots, magical for children, of honey, apricot and strawberry jams, eaten at white clothed tables lighted by maroon shaded lamps. Those dining cars were the nationalised successors to the pre-ordered picnic baskets delivered to passengers in pre-war days and precursors to the return of Trollope's disappointing sandwiches on the buffets and trolleys of our re-privatized railways, where the death knell has lately sounded over even the few remaining First Class dining cars.

Icy cold, the obligatory slice of ham, beef or chicken, hummus for vegetarians, all tasting, in spite of the 'mustard mayonnaise' and the 'fresh horseradish', of little beyond slightly rancid lettuce, lain too long with stringy tomato in plastic enveloped bread whose taste has long since dissipated. Multi-flavoured crisps, millionaire's shortbread or miserable flapjacks with eternal sell by dates; there is little excitement or enjoyment to be found amongst the gloomy packets that make up today's pre-packaged train picnics on regular services that offer only rare and expensive dining car alternatives.

For the more leisured and wealthy traveller there are exclusive gourmet train journeys; on the Blue Train in South Africa; the Wine Train in Napa Valley, California; the trains of the Orient Express company in Europe or the UK and the various 'Palaces on Wheels' in India. These provide serious restaurant food, too much and too often one sometimes hears, and a very different pleasure to the 'train meals' of the early 20th Century described by Constance Spry as 'of the nature of picnics'.

> 'I well remember the first time I had a luncheon basket on a train: ordered ahead by wire it was brought to the carriage at some main-line station en route. Now, I thought, I really am grown up, no more packets of sandwiches for me. Someone must have tipped the guard, for I remember he brought in a fresh footwarmer and inquired if I was comfortable. Hair up, long skirts, luncheon basket, the Strand Magazine, on my way to my first house party – I was beginning life. In the basket was a wing of chicken, roll, butter, biscuits, cheese and, I think, celery and possibly cake or a jam tart and an apple, and I have an idea that it cost 2s 6d, though it may have been less'.

The luncheon basket came in various guises and prices. From Chester station in 1876, 'The Aristocrat', including for 5/-, chicken, ham or tongue, bread, cheese and either a pint of claret or half a pint of sherry – followed by a cracking headache one can't help but think. 'The Democrat' offered cold meat or pie, bread and cheese with a mere pint bottle of ale or stout. In 1884 the Midland Railway provided a 'hot basket' but problems with the 'hot' description seem to have been responsible for the idea never really taking on. As dining cars on trains became more frequent and able to provide sustenance of better quality and value than the questionable contents of luncheon or tea baskets, their popularity waned, although the system only ceased altogether as food and staff shortages began to bite in 1941.

On Trains and Aeroplanes

This 1912 rhyme by a railway apprentice parodying Omar Khayyam suggests that Ms Spry's memory may have had more to do with hindsight and that footwarmer than the contents of her basket.

A Loaf of Bread, a Cup of Wine, and thou
Beside me on the cushion, and I trow
The Railway train is paradise enow.

When from old age she's disincline to lay,
The hen from earth is quickly called away;
Whither her Spirit goes I cannot say.

But this I know, if anyone should ask it,
Her body, or as poets say, her casket
Reposes in the Railway Luncheon Basket.

Behold the leg that wandered once at will,
With some pin feathers clinging to it still'
How thin it looks bedecked with paper frill.

The breast, unruffled now by love or care,
Looks keen and sharp when of its plumage bare;
'Twill cut your fingers if you don't take care.

Now she will quickly travel down the line,
Companioned by a bottle of bad wine,
And doubtful slice of ham, cut very fine.

And, if for further luxuries you seek,
A piece of cheese, decidedly antique,
And roll that's left the oven for a week.

Come, traveler, undo the basket's strap,
And place the savoury mess upon your lap;
You have my sympathy, my poor, dear chap.

For if upon the ancient bird you dine,
Or finish up that dose of shilling wine,
You have a keener appetite than mine.

(Dinner and the Diner - The History of Railway Catering)

A later train picnic enjoyed by Constance was, we note, made by a 'family member'. It sounds beautifully planned, quite simple but luxurious, seasonal and perfect enough for the most discerning eater at Glyndebourne or Ascot then or now.

This was for 'a small party going up to the far north':

> 'Each of us was handed when we got into our sleepers a small, neat cardboard box containing two little screw-top cartons and other small packages. In one carton was a perfectly freshly made lobster salad in a delicious dressing, the second carton contained fresh fruit salad of peaches, strawberries and orange. Crisp poppy-seed rolls were quartered and buttered, and a Porosan bag held the crisp heart of a cos lettuce. There were small cream cheese rolls made by taking two short pieces of celery, filling the hollow made when they were put together with cream cheese, and rolling the whole in brown bread and butter.'

Elizabeth David was passionate about properly made mayonnaise but not to the extent of considering it always the best sauce for a cold dish, even lobster. As she says, 'most cold lobster sauces, including mayonnaise, are on the heavy side for what is already rich and solid food'. Her sauce for 'Lobster Courchamps' is a perfect picnic dressing.

Railway Lamb Curry
Serves 4-6
(Curries and Bugles)

The bones from a shoulder of lamb (or mutton); 2 inch piece of fresh ginger root; ½ teaspoon salt; 6 small red chilies, seeded and chopped; 7 cloves of garlic, smashed, peeled and chopped; 1 teaspoon cumin seeds; 2 tablespoons coriander seeds; ½ teaspoon ground turmeric; 3 tablespoons ghee; 1 large onion, peeled and finely chopped; 6 curry leaves; 1lb boned shoulder of lamb (mutton), trimmed of fat and cut into 1 inch cubes; 2 large potatoes, peeled and cut into 1 inch cubes; 6 fl oz coconut milk; 4 tablespoons tamarind liquid; 1 teaspoon salt.

Make a concentrated stock from the lamb bones, half the ginger and the salt – use enough water to cover the bones and then simmer until stock is reduced to about 8fl oz. Strain and reserve. While the stock is boiling, place the remaining ginger, the chilies and garlic in a processor or mortar and process or pound to a paste. Grind or pound the cumin and coriander seeds to a powder and add them to the paste, together with the turmeric. Add a teaspoon of water to mix the paste thoroughly. Melt the ghee in a large saucepan over medium heat and fry the onion and curry leaves, stirring constantly, until the onion is soft. Add the spice paste from the last step and stir and fry it for 3 minutes. Then pour in the stock, bring to the boil and add the meat, potatoes and coconut milk. Reduce the heat and let the curry simmer, uncovered, for at least 30 minutes, or until the lamb and potatoes are tender. The gravy should have reduced and thickened also by this time. Add the tamarind water and season with the salt. Serve with plain rice and perhaps a dhal to accompany it. The curry will taste even better if it is made the day before and re-heated.

The Indian Viceroys had their own train to take them and their vast staff on their biannual tours round the country. In 1907 there were drawbacks even to the most luxurious train travel as Lady Minto, the Vicereine, reported in her journal:

> Our journey through the Scinde desert seemed like a voyage in the infernal regions. In spite of electric fans, the thermometer was 90° in our carriages, and the whole of the dust of desert seemed to penetrate through every aperture, eyes, nose, and mouth seemed full of it, and thick layers of dust covered us from

head to foot. At meals the drinks were thoroughly iced, but the glasses felt so hot to one's lips that it was quite disagreeable touching them. The train stopped for dinner, and the windows being open, all the insects of the desert were attracted by the light. Locusts innumerable alighted on our faces and hands, springing with marvellous agility from person to person, and caused a most disagreeable diversion during our evening meal. The Staff made a large collection which would no doubt be of great value to an etymological museum. The dinner was a noisy one, many and varied screams frequently rent the air, as none of the family can be calm under the determined attack of an army of insects. The climax was reached when an enormous sort of flying frog suddenly alighted on Colonel Dunlop's shirt front. With great valour he caught the animal, in spite of a severe sting. It was hastily drowned in whiskey, and the scientists of Quetta are endeavouring to discover to what species it belongs. It was the most revolting object I have ever seen — a large scaly back, gigantic antiller, very long legs and feet composed of spreading brown coral, rather like cauliflower leaves. Had such a creature alighted on me, I doubt my still being in possession of my senses.'

On a long journey from Bombay to Trivandrum our vast insulated 48 hours worth of picnic was disdained by the children in favour of railway food and the sweets, biscuits and fruit generously and unendingly supplied by fellow passengers. Travel in India is a social affair and the hours of long train journeys spent in close proximity slip quickly by in conversation, shared food and oblivious sleep. A foreigner is always the focus of particular attention and memories of sometimes surreal conversations woven over chai and the proffered biscuit packet fuel the pens of travel writers, especially the grand master of train travel, Paul Theroux, to whom every new companion in the sleeper compartment is meat and drink.

His companion on the Rajdhani Express heading for Bombay, Mr Radia, sits reading *Blitz* magazine, the gossipy scandal sheet that feeds the Bollywood dream with gleeful reports and glossy photographs of celebrity excess.

Russian winter brought further disaster to Napoleon and the French army suffered hiccups in their supply lines in World War 1. British soldiers have, however, struggled more than most against apathetic, parsimonious, central regulation and vague, often unsubstantiated expectations, of paternalistic generosity towards their men from the officers of individual regiments.

Octogenarian William Henry Hare's memoir of life as a young Ensign of the 51st Regiment of Foot during the retreat to Corunna in 1808/09 suggests that officers certainly had an interest in the quality of their own victuals. Ensign Hare was also interested in his surroundings, commenting on the 'splendid garden' full of orange and lemon trees attached to the monastery in St Iago de Compostela where the officers were billeted and the 'fine old city' of Astorga, much damaged by the French. The whole army, however, was desperately short of food, lack of forage forced the destruction of most of the horses and pack mules and the chaos grew as the raggle taggle soldiery scoured the surrounding country for sustenance.

On Christmas Day in Astorga:

> 'Three brother officers and myself had clubbed together and had got a half starved turkey which we bought at the village the day before, and we bought of the woman of the house some sausages which she fried. They were tolerable excepting for the quantity of Garlic which we could not get rid of for days from our taste and smell.'

Whether Hare's memories were gilded by the glow of a happy old age, he seems determined to have seen the glass half full, finding 'very tolerable' also the men's mixture of flour and slices of fat pork (this would have been the salted pork ration in the absence of beef) cooked on the top of mess tins. A few days later as the retreat 'now became a regular rout with complete disorganization consequent on the absence of any commissariat supplies', Hare found himself cold and wet, making the best of things in a loft when he received this welcome invitation:

Picnic Crumbs

'My Dear William,
I find you are in the shed opposite me. I have got some hot soup and a bit of mutton. My brigade Major and I are just going to sit down to, and enough for you.
Yours,
George Cookson'
(Ensign William Henry Hare, *Archives of National Army Museum*)

It took the horrific conditions of the Crimean war and the great Reform Club chef Alexis Soyer, a Frenchman of course, to begin changes in the way army food was prepared. It was far longer before successive disinterested governments were energized to create a centralised system for the improvement of quantity and quality of rations. Part of the problem seems to have been the British soldier's own lack of care for the cooking and taste of the monotonous bully beef and bread or biscuit that would have been execrable to his French colleagues, who, as Soyer said, all 'understand a little cooking'. The soldiers ration, set in 1813 at ¾ pound meat and 1 pound of bread per day, was the same at the end of the Boer War. In 1864, years after the Crimea, the French soldiers' ration included vegetables, wine and brandy, while the British built and lost an empire fuelled mainly by tea and beer and whatever additional edibles the more enterprising could beg, borrow or steal.

In a letter written from Varna, the base for the Anglo-French force operating against the Russians at Sevastopol in the Crimea, Private John Rose of the 50th Regiment commented on the expectation of an easy victory and the abominable rations.

'We have been living on 1 pound and a half of brown bread and 1 pound of meat per day but it is not fit for men to use so some times we use it and other times we bury it'.

(Letter written by Pte John Rose, 50th Regiment, to his parents.
Varna, 28th Aug 1854).

An old friend of mine, then a very young officer fighting his way up Italy with the allies, was every bit as enterprising in the pursuit of food and as determined, too, to find the food he enjoyed. He had very clear likes and dislikes, as I well know after years of being educated about good and bad food when staying with his family while I was growing up. He would travel for miles to collect the best cheese, bread, meat, or to buy and try something new that he had heard was particularly good and should be tested. Only certain suppliers were up to the task and this must equally have been the case in wartime, judging by the diary of one of his fellow officers in 1944, even in the most makeshift field accommodation.

> 18th May: Bobs, Tony and I are living in a shelter of tarpaulin up the hill.
> Wednesday 24th May: Bobs got up at 5.30 and went to Naples before breakfast to get asparagus.'
> It is hard to imagine that the following lunch was also cooked under the tarpaulin – perhaps things had improved by then.
> 'Thursday 17th August: Roast duck and chocolate soufflé made by Bobs for lunch.

This is Marcel Boulestin's Soufflé au Chocolat. Greatly admired by Elizabeth David, his precise manner of describing food and cooking, his appreciation of good ingredients, reminds me of Bobs. He makes the soufflé sound hardy enough too, to stand up to battle zone cooking.

For this soufflé, as indeed for most soufflés, the proportion of eggs is two to each person. There are a great many mistaken ideas in connection with this delicious dish, one of them being that if you open the door of the oven it becomes flat at once; in fact a soufflé cannot be made by exact timing, and you must watch it carefully to see if it is getting on as it should be, quickly enough, yet not too quickly. Of course you must not leave the door of the oven open or open it too much, but you must not be afraid to glance at it if necessary. This chocolate soufflé is specially light, as it does not contain any flour at all.

Soufflé au Chocolat

Grate about a handful of pure cocoa, add a good deal of castor sugar (pure cocoa is very bitter), put in six yolks of egg and melt slowly over the fire, stirring well. See that it is sweet enough and smooth. Put away to cool while you beat the six whites to a stiff froth, when they are ready add them to the chocolate mixture, put in half first and mix, then the rest and mix again. The mixing should be done with a light hand.

Put the finished article in the soufflé dish, which you have previously greased, with a little butter and sprinkled with sugar.

Cook and serve at once.

The war in the Western desert offered fewer possibilities for luxury scrounging although Mike Peyton in his memoir describes one unexpected bonus feast, a distinct improvement on the normal tinned bully beef and hard tack biscuits with their habitual seasoning of sand.

> 'I've heard men say, just as they would of salt, "It needs a bit more sand in it," and, bending down, they would take a pinch of sand and sprinkle it in their bully stew. It wouldn't make any noticeable difference.
>
> It was my turn to cook and what was on offer was the normal tins of bully or a large piece of meat. It was large because no one else had wanted it and it wasn't difficult to see why. When one shone a flashlight on it, it was for all the world like a huge lump of black rubber. The inside looked as meat should, red and bloody. There were only four of us to cook for at that time so I could afford to waste some. When it came time to cook this hunk of meat I sliced off all the black outer layer and cut the rest into mouth-sized chunks and put it in the Dixie with some tinned vegetables and left it on the Tommy Cooker while we got on with whatever was the job in hand... What lifted it out of the ordinary was that, just as we were going to eat it, we got the order to move. The only thing I could do with the

this beautiful and costly fabric. He finds, besides, the carpets, expensive but much to his liking, excellent cloth for hard-wearing shooting suits and gold work only spoilt by the jewellers determined use of 'Streeter's Machine-made Jewellery' catalogue as his design inspiration. Less pleasing to contemporary sensibilities are his shooting exploits, encompassing the unfortunate and rather too regular wounding of animals so rare today that we stalk them only with a camera and a lot of luck. Nonetheless 19th century sportsmen in pursuit of trophies were secure in their additional fulfilment of a suitably paternalistic responsibility to the local populace by ridding them of dangerous pests and, while a left and right of bears was a thrilling excess, Mr Lambert is a little shamefaced over the death of an old female bear whose cub escaped 'howling like a puppy', no doubt to die of starvation.

> 'There has apparently been little diminution in the numbers of black bears and their depredations cause serious injury to the crops. In 1871, four officers of one regiment carried away eighty skins, of which nearly half fell to one man's rifle. Most of the bears of Kashmir have been fired at, and near villages their temper is not of the best. The people believe that black bears sometimes carry off women into the forests, and they speak of their wonderful ingenuity – how they tie up rushes to form a shady bower, and how they sometimes tie up female bears.'

By 1895 the brown or red bears, Lambert's target, were, perhaps unsurprisingly, 'greatly diminished in numbers though still reasonably populous. The red bear is partly herbivorous and partly carnivorous and many cattle are killed every year by red bears. Length up to and slightly over seven feet.'

Lambert was more graphically interested in his prey than his stomach unlike some of his contemporaries. Nevertheless, the division of his party and their supplies into two groups was a discomfiting process and he noted the necessity of tossing a coin for a pot of marmalade against a tin of sardines among other essential and indissoluble provisions. Some solace for the loss of the marmalade, an important centre to the Victorian sportsman's breakfast, may have been forthcoming in a local gift of 'six pounds of dried apricots, which were promptly turned into excellent jam by our Khansaman'.

Bears in India are more likely to eat man than vice versa and I doubt the English hunter valued his prey for the pot although in more northern parts of the world, Alaska, Canada, Finland and the Baltic States in particular, bear meat continues to be a delicacy. No doubt the former Republican Vice-Presidential candidate, Sarah Palin, has an index full of recipes for bear meat. Internet sites for hunters abound with recipes for sausages, stews and bear meat loaf. Along with recipes for squirrel, 'cut 2 plump young squirrels into serving pieces', muskrat and groundhog, *The Gourmet Cookbook* published in New York in 1950, has several for bear, including Bear Steak Alexandre I, a recipe which, with its Worcestershire sauce and mustard, is of a very similar format to recipes for the camp food enjoyed by colonial sportsmen and other travellers.

Bear Steak

'Marinate a 41/2 pound slice of bear loin for at least 24 hours and dry it well. Rub a mashed clove of garlic on a heated platter. Make a paste of 3 tablespoons of butter, 3 tablespoons of finely minced chives, 1 generous teaspoon of mustard, 11/2 tablespoons tomato paste, and a dash of Worcestershire sauce. Cover the platter with this paste and add a thick layer of onion smothered in butter. Season with ½ teaspoon salt, pepper, and a little paprika. Keep the platter hot. Sear the steak well on both sides under a high flame and broil the meat as desired, basting frequently with melted butter. Dust the steak with salt and pepper and serve on the platter, topped with mushroom caps sautéed in brown butter and sprinkled with chopped parsley.'

The 1870s produced a wealth of travel books and stories from around the world, adding reports of less familiar and less rosy regions to descriptions and enjoyment of local ingredients, is apparent in recipe books and accounts of menus, especially in camp and when travelling. Emily Eden wrote in 1839 of the food provided for her brother's camp, to the irritation of his French chef, by the King of Oude. 'Some of the dishes are very good, though too strongly spiced and perfumed for English tastes. They make up some dishes with assafoetida!* but we stick to the rice and pilaus and curries'. (*Up the Country*)

Emma Roberts, accompanying her sister and brother-in-law around India earlier in the 19th century, the 1830s, views camp food with the same optimistic pleasure and interested eye as she turns upon all aspects of Indian life in her *Scenes and Characteristics of Hindostan*. She comments favourably upon dishes invented to suit portable cooking facilities: 'A *burdwan* stew ranks high amongst these concoctions and two sauces which go under the name of *shikarree* (hunters) and camp-sauce, are assuredly the most piquant adjuncts to flesh and fowl which the genius of a gastronome has ever compounded'. For hunting parties she recommends painted snipe as a good stand in for the familiar woodcock of the north and home; jungle fowl for pheasant; rock partridge and a variety of pigeons to make 'not only an exhilarating, but a very interesting meal. The most elaborate *pic-nic* provided for a *fete champetre* in England, where people are put to all sorts of inconveniences, and must content themselves with a cold collation, is nothing to the luxurious displays of cookery performed in the open air in India.'

---

* Asafoetida was better known in Europe at the time as an ill-smelling root with medicinal properties – the French called it *merde du diable*

Two methods for Burdwan Stew

Take either cold rabbit, fowl, veal, or lamb, and having cut it into pieces, put it into a pan over a lamp, with as much good gravy as will cover it: add a piece of butter rolled in flour, an onion shred fine, two spoonsful of essence of anchovy, a glass of port wine, cayenne and salt: stew slowly for a quarter of an hour.
(The London Art of Cookery and Domestic Housekeepers' Complete Assistance)

Cut into joints a cold fowl or duck; put it into s stew-pan with half a pint of gravy, a large wine-glass of ale, half a one of white wine, the juice of half a lemon, a tea-spoonful of soy and cayenne; of mushroom catsup, lemon pickle, cucumber vinegar, corach escavecke, a dessert-spoonful each. Heat all thoroughly before serving. Cold boiled or roasted lamb or kid may be dressed in this way.
(The Practice of Cookery adapted to the business of every day life)

Hobson Jobson, the dictionary of Anglo-Indian vocabulary, throws little light on the stew. The town of Burdwan or Bardhaman, West Bengal, 67 miles north of Calcutta was, however, a district headquarters in British India and it seems reasonable to think that travellers between the two might have so named their regular camp stew.

"Our" Camp Cake
from Camp Recipes for Camp People by 'Chota Sahib'

Half a quart bottle of ghee, 1lb of flour, 8 eggs, ¾ lb of bazaar sugar (1st sort), a handful of plums, a handful of almonds, a few drops of essence of lemon and a glass of brandy; put the ghee in a basin and stir in the flour slowly; add the sugar, plums and almonds and mix these thoroughly well together; beat the eggs and add to them the brandy; add these to the cake, with a few drops of essence of lemon; keep stirring for 15 minutes, and put into a lined tin and bake thoroughly. This cake will keep good for a month.

'Chota Sahib' suggests cutlets of well-spiced pounded liver, garnished with fried parsley and a 'nice gravy' made, rather inevitably, with sherry, anchovy and Worcestershire sauce as suitable camp food. These are to be fashioned with a piece of toasted crust to imitate the bone of a chop and remind me of the delicious 'lobster cutlets' we ate as children in Scotland with a piece of macaroni serving as the fake bone.

Mrs MacNeill's Lobster or Salmon Cutlets

Break up cooked lobster or flake salmon with fingers and add to a nice white sauce, well seasoned. Add a dash of tomato ketchup for colour and leave in frig until cold. Shape into cutlets; flour, egg and breadcrumb. Fry in hot oil and insert a piece of macaroni to imitate a cutlet bone. Serve with fried parsley and lemon quarters or with fresh tomato sauce.

Sir Francis Colchester Wemyss, author of *Pleasures of the Table*, was born a Victorian and died an Elizabethan. His interest in food was developed during his Indian army years when, like others of his fellows, his attempts to get the food he wanted to eat encouraged closer involvement in the process of its cooking. He began a two month leave pig-sticking in India in the latter years of the 19th century with less than promising provisions; by the time he and his young fellow officers had bought their horses, the only meat they could afford was a dozen tins of condemned bully beef but it sounds as if their game bag sustained them successfully as he remarks that they 'did very well living on the country'.

T. Earle Welby, author of *The Dinner Knell and Away, Dull Cookery*, not to mention a life of Swinburne and a study of the Victorian Romantics, was a journalist in India for much of his life. Elizabeth David considers his 'Shooters Sandwich' 'invaluable' for picnics and journeys.

want food, or at any rate not our food; they simply formed a circle round us at a respectful distance and stared and howled.

First we pretended not to notice, then we shoo-ed them away several times. They returned immediately, with reinforcements, re-formed their dreadful circle, and howled and stared and sniffed again, until they forced us to get into our cars and return to the city, leaving them in possession of their ruin.'   (*Summer Food*)

Jaffrey's picnic was an Indian scale joint family affair:

'The entire family went on the picnic. During my childhood, it did not occur to me that families could come in sizes smaller than thirty people, swelling beatifically to a few thousand at the mere hint of a wedding.'

Those 30 people piled into two cars would progress through the city and the multiple layers of Delhi history, disgorging breathless ladies in crumpled saris, tall men, servants, and all the baskets and pots of meats and potatoes, *pooris* and pickles, to be arranged on carpets and cloths while the children raced to the top of the tower:

'From the top of the tower, we children could survey all the other Delhis – the thirteenth-century Delhi of the Khilji dynasty, the fourteenth-century fort of the Tughlak dynasty, the fifteenth-century tomb of the Moghul emperor Humanun, Shah Jahan's seventeenth-century mosque, and then British India with its elegant avenues and round shopping centre.

Soon our eyes, impelled by our stomachs, would settle on something closer – the sight of a brightly edged cotton duree over which hovered some very familiar short ladies. We would think of the meatballs cooked with cumin, coriander and yohfurt and the juicy mangoes cooling in tubs of ice....and we would all come thundering down the hundreds of steps.'

(*A Taste of India*)

bottle of large black French plums, or better still, a basket of fresh fruit costing what your purse can buy or your fruit room produce, a handful of glacé ginger cubes or a tin of peppermint creams, and lastly the cup of hot coffee, black or white, tasting as good out of the Thermos as tea tastes nasty. And though there is no fire, there can yet be smoke of cigarette, cigar, or pipe, to taste.

Now comes the moment for a gentle *promenade de digestion*, or stretch across open country with a motor rendezvous at the end, for enjoying the scenery of local architecture, for taking intelligent interest in Roman camp or prehistoric remains, for noting the birds and sharing your food with them, for descending, like the prophet's ravens, with the surplus of your feast, on the nearest road-menders or country children, remembering to ask their acceptance thereof with all the courtesy you can command. Perhaps before you turn homewards you will collect a few delicate trails of ivy, better taken than left, from some wayside trees, to float in your flat bowl, or a bunch of late autumn foliage or winter evergreen to gladden your town home more intimately than florists' trophies. The nursery might be made happy by a sod of growing daisies from the hedgerow, such as have given great poets thoughts too deep for tears, and which could fill the empty luncheon receptacles, only forbearing to damage wild beauty which is everybody's possession. Such a day might well hold more material comfort and bodily invigoration, more imaginative suggestion as well as some saving to sorely-tried purses, than the hours often spent in stuffy public dining rooms and crowded hotel lounges, for in the words of Meredith, 'when we let Romance go, we change the sky for a ceiling.'

(Kitchen Essays: With Recipes and Their Occasions)

and occasionally joining with the cook in the practical details of the manufacture of the much-praised dish. Then they returned to the upper regions, flushed but victorious, and the dish was the dinner — or the main feature of it — for the evening. It was a glorious success, but there was just one little drawback. The garlic had predominated so strongly that no one save the two *chefs* themselves could venture upon tasting it. The upshot of it all was that Wilkie went home and took to his bed, while my father remained at home and took to his. They were both very ill for several days, with a horrible gastric attack, and garlic was never more mentioned in the house.'*

While the extravagantly themed parties, given by the great hostesses and decorators like Syrie Maugham and Elsie de Wolfe, continued during the 1930s, the hyperbole of society cookery books reduced. In descriptions of food for travelling in particular, Lady Jekyll's fantastic picnic directives and Hilda Leyel's marvellously inventive recipes from *The Gentle Art of Cookery* gave way to suitably practical suggestions in her 1936 *Picnics for Motorists*. The gathering clouds of austerity still allowed for a foie gras pie but her note that it is both expensive and ambitious discourages; the inclusion of a pound of truffles makes it sound impossibly sybaritic today.

Mrs Leyel recommends the 'wide mouthed thermos flask' for curries and soups both hot and cold but her statement that 'The art of arranging cold meals is to choose dishes that are better cold than they would be hot' is somewhat belied by several recipes that could not possibly be so. I am unconvinced by a 'Cold Liver Loaf' or cold 'Excellent Fish Pie', a sort of kedgeree under a pastry crust, even with a salsa-like uncooked 'cold catsup'. Cold pheasant is fine if usually dry and one can't help feeling that the opening of a pot of cold bread sauce to help it down is unlikely to be met with cries of joy. Elizabeth David, for whom Mrs Leyel was an early inspiration, did not, unlike her, favour dishes in aspic, melting away on a warm day. Some of the recipes would undoubtedly do better indoors but there are plenty of transportable and unusual salads and soups,

---

* Nathaniel Thomas Beard was the younger son of Francis Carr Beard, Wilkie's doctor and friend for much of his life. Nathaniel Beard was later chief clerk at Bentley's publishing house. Beard's *Some Recollections of Yesterday* published in the periodical *Temple Bar* in 1894 includes six pages of childhood memories of Collins' visits to the family home at 44 Welbeck St.

and a chocolate mousse, if improbable picnic food, is always going to be acceptable if it survives the journey.

I like horseradish and Mrs Leyel likes it in her salad dressings which make very ordinary ingredients a lot more interesting. She grates it over a green pea and ham salad, otherwise dressed simply with oil and vinegar and uses the cooked salad dressing for this pea and potato salad and another of beetroot and celery.

Horseradish, Pea and Potato Salad

Choose waxy potatotes, cook them and chop them into small pieces; cook some green peas and let them drain well, and freely shred a stick or more of horseradish.

Then put the peas and potato into a salad bowl and mix the horseradish with it. Cover with the following sauce:

Beat two eggs in a double saucepan, add a saltspoonful of salt, a teaspoonful of mixed mustard, two dessertspoonsful of sugar, an ounce of butter, four tablespoonfuls of milk and three tablespoonfuls of vinegar.

Stir until thick and then pour over the salad.

Elizabeth David's own memory of a pre World War 2 picnic with American acquaintances while visiting friends in France is a story of dashed expectations.

'It was agreed that the two parties should proceed in their own cars to a little bay outside Marseille, and that we should each bring our own provisions. On Sunday morning I and my friends indulged in a delicious hour of shopping in the wonderful market of the rue de Rome, buying olives, in 1974, picnics in a nearby square were the order for lunch throughout the summer. Not surprisingly they sound quite delicious; a tian, home-made bread, cheese, and the all important wine. The bottle was attached with string to a convenient bush and lowered into the central pool in the square to cool during the morning's work. Amazingly it never got stolen.

Elizabeth David was inspired by Hilda Leyel who considered wine a most important adjunct to food.

> 'Nowadays, when French wine is to be had for two shilling a bottle, it is a pity that the northern nations do not emulate the southern races and drink more wine. The light wines of France or Spain are more wholesome than spirits or than the strangely concocted cocktails with weird names that come from America.
>
> Why is it that drinking is so much more poetical than eating? Homer wrote lyrically about "sweet honey-hearted wine," but the rebuke of Antinous to Odysseus, whom he accuses of being "wounded with the honey-sweet wine" that "taken in great draughts and drunk out of measure darkened the mind and the heart of Eurytion, so that he wrought foul deed and began the war between the Centaurs and manking," is far more poetical than any modern temperance literature, and no less convincing.'

(Elizabeth Kent quotes the *Girl's Own Paper* in her book *Picnic Basket;* the Claret Cup recipe is Mrs Leyel's)

Claret Cup

Wrap the ice in a blanket and put it under the seat of the wagon. Claret cup is sure to be wanted, to be mixed on the spot by one of the men of the party. I have noticed that when a man has made a claret cup which is appreciated he feels thoroughly satisfied and at peace with the world in general.

Put into a bowl the very thin rind of a lemon, a little sugar, and a wineglassful of sherry. Add a bottle of claret, sugar to taste, a spring of lemon-scented verbena, one bottle of aerated water, and a grated nutmeg. Strain and ice. (A whole grated nutmeg is a lot for one bottle only of claret – it is safer to grate and taste as you go along) larger and more democratic audience. Monuments of earlier seasons like the Eton Harrow cricket match still continue but without the social hullabaloo of the past. More recent additions to the summer round, the opera at Glyndebourne, founded in 1934, and its more recent imitators, have added to the number of excuses for latter day Fête champêtres and contemporary picnic one-upmanship. Things got out of hand a few years ago at the 4th of June at Eton, the historical celebration of George III's birthday and a day when parents and their sons picnic on the sports fields. The past high society connotations of a private school event were revived as the exclusive bait for corporate entertaining by opportunist outsiders with marquees, an innovation unsurprisingly deplored by the headmaster. The headmaster at my sons' old style preparatory school was outraged when a misguided parent appeared on Sports Day with a small tent and a large barbecue; typical picnic food on rugs on the cricket pitch followed by a spectacular school tea were the proper and expected order of the day.

The committed sportsperson may always have had reservations about turning an important event into a social occasion. Alfred E. T. Watson, in a 1903 critique of Henley as a venue for international competition, comments: '- the course is not suited for it. In the first place it is too short; in the second place it is too crowded with pleasure boats, and, if I may use the word, is too picnicky.' (Alfred Edward Thomas Watson, *English Sport*)

The sport versus picnic problem has not improved in these days when no one can survive a short walk without bottles of mineral water and/or additional sustenance. In June 2009, the following letter appeared in the *Daily Telegraph* from disgruntled of St Leonards-on-Sea:

> 'While trying to enjoy a day out at the Centre Court at Wimbledon this week, we were continuously disrupted by so-called tennis fans rustling plastic bags, opening food containers and chewing, gulping and occasionally burping while indulging in their culinary delights.
> I had always assumed that the Wimbledon courts were an arena to watch tennis and not a place to have an afternoon picnic.

> The Lawn Tennis Association should prohibit the annoying and distracting consumption of food within the main courts. There are numerous areas in the grounds to enjoy a picnic. After all, the players demand a quiet environment while playing, so why can't the spectators while watching.'

At the Queen's tournament this year, the noise from surrounding eaters was less of a problem than the sight, why do other people's packed lunches look so dissimilar to anything one would wish to eat oneself? Years ago when the international tennis tournament in Hong Kong was one of the major occasions of the year we used to have quite silent and, I hope, reasonably elegant picnics; tiny cucumber, ham or tomato sandwiches; very good white wine, admittedly in paper cups – light weight and no clinking; and flasks of deliciously flavoured consommé, drunk from the same disposable vessels.

These days most entertainment and sporting venues bustle with food outlets and the proper picnic, as opposed to the impromptu audience snack, may seem too much time, trouble, and too reliant on unpredictable weather. The social picnic, where it does happen, may be at least as competitive as the event in hand, whether for its home made perfection or as a demonstration of money-no-object professional catering. Remembering shivering over the sandwiches in a drizzly car park at Royal Ascot, I have complete sympathy with those who think the effort versus pleasure ratio unequal; at the same time, an interval picnic in the gardens at Glyndebourne on a beautiful evening remains one of the great pleasures of an English summer.

This description of a 19th century Goodwood Cup Day at the summer Goodwood race meeting, the traditional end of the social Season, sounds horribly familiar:

> A couple of races of no great importance are run, races with which social Goodwood, unless friends own competitors, have little to do. Luncheon time is coming, and with many anxious glances upwards from kindly hosts and hostesses, to say nothing of hungry guests, parties are arranging themselves

round hospitable tablecloths. If on the beech leaves overhead the raindrops should begin to patter down, lunch is of course ruined. Into the champagne glasses they drip, and by no means improve the delicate flavour of the '74 Perrier Jouet; the Mayonnaise presently assumes a spotty appearance. Leaves fall from the flowers which tasteful luxury provides in water glasses as at a dinner-table; a moisture not its own is given to the pigeon pie; and a sort of rain gravy forms in dishes of cold chicken; ladies pull up the hoods of their ulsters, men turn up their collars, umbrellas spring up all down the beeches like a growth of magical mushrooms.

(Alfred Edward Thomas Watson, *Racecourse and Covert Side*)

Judging by the memories of Glyndebourne kept in its archives, picnics there have always been variable feasts although champagne has a regular role. Wonderful though these alfresco dinners may be, there is no doubt that it is easier to eat, safe from the elements, in the restaurants but it does rather take away the romance.

SUMMER 1958

I was a young fellow working in London, and I had two tickets in the Gods, bought months in advance, for My Fair Lady. My flat-mate at the time was seriously courting a young woman whose father owned several thousand acres of East Anglia, and who was desperate to see My Fair Lady.
'All right,' I said finally, 'you can have my tickets, but in return I want two tickets for Glyndebourne.'
'Done,' he said.
Working in Baker Street at the time, I flogged along at lunch time to Ibbs and Tillet, who ran Glyndebourne's London box office. They offered me two stall tickets for Le Comte Ory which set me back six pounds the pair (twice the price of my Drury Lane tickets).

In those days, when one only had two weeks holiday a year, the next problem was to find someone with whom I could escape from London for a few hours on a midweek afternoon. I remembered Jenny.

Jenny was a model with gorgeous red hair, and, yes, she would love to come. She had heard of Glyndebourne, which was rather unusual in those days amongst the girls I usually went out with, but, like me had never been there. I told her we would take a picnic – I would bring champagne and she volunteered to bring the food.

Came the interval and we returned to the car park to collect our picnic. On the way back I saw Jenny looking at some of the picnic rugs on which smoked salmon and asparagus were appearing.

'I'm afraid,' she said apologetically as she produced a brown paper bag from her shopping basket.

'Looks lovely,' I said, wondering what it contained. 'Let's find somewhere to sit."

I think we ended up by the lake, though, after fifty years, it's hard to be sure. I dug out the champagne, popped the cork and filled our glasses. Meanwhile Jenny busied herself with her brown bag, which contained a packet neatly wrapped in grease proof paper.

'I'm sorry,' she began again. 'I had no idea it was like this – '

'Please,' I reassured her. I raised my glass to her.

Slowly she unwrapped the grease proof paper and exposed four tomato sandwiches. How we laughed. Champagne and tomato sandwiches!

(Anon. Glyndebourne)

Arabella Boxer, the author of the famous *First Slice your Cookbook* (a book where each page is cut horizontally into three for easy assembly of different menus that can be viewed in one spread), understands from longer experience what is expected of a Glyndebourne picnic.

'A totally different sort of picnic that occurs, though less frequently, in my life is the evening picnic. An expedition to Glyndebourne is a good example of this sort of occasion, and here it seems worthwhile to be more extravagant. I like to construct this sort of picnic as if it were a formal meal, served on china plates with proper silver and glass, taking a pretty tablecloth to spread on the grass. Several bottles of chilled white wine, or even better, still champagne, are almost obligatory. To start, perhaps home-made potted shrimps with small sandwiches of brown bread and butter, or giant prawns or crayfish, served with mayonnaise. The possibly some small chicken pies, served warm; or a roll of flaky pastry enclosing a large spicy sausage served with a mustard sauce; or an enclosed quiche, like a shallow pie, filled with spinach and tomatoes, or mushrooms, fish and rice. An alternative menu might consist of a hot consommé madrilène or a bortsch served in small cups and followed by a cold main dish such as smoked chicken or turkey, cold duck, or a duck pâté with crusty French bread and a green salad. Slices of cold roast sirloin can be rolled round small heaps of freshly grated horseradish, or thick slices of rare fillet of beef can be served with a rich and creamy horseradish sauce.'

She recommends a tin of chocolate brownies as an easy pudding.

It sounds delicious, if the rain stays away. Dozing off after a good dinner and 'several bottles of white wine', not to mention pre-performance Pimms, is another hazard although the latest, air-conditioned theatre at Glyndebourne has reduced the problem. In the old, cramped and close space, programmes swished constantly in a vain effort to stir the air. One man had a heart attack in the front row and was quietly removed as the music played on and a woman in a daffodil yellow dress crumpled to the floor during the interval cutting her head on the stone steps.

I am never convinced about home-made potted shrimps given the general taste for the bought variety but the idea is appealing and more so now you can buy plastic boxes of fresh shelled brown shrimps. Shelling them yourself is a thoroughly unrewarding chore and larger shrimps just aren't the same.

Arabella Boxer's potted shrimps

- 360g shelled cooked shrimps
- 240g butter
- ½ bay leaf
- Pinch of gound mace
- Coarsely ground black pepper

Cut the butter in pieces and melt it. Add the bay leaf and mace and leave for 5 minutes. Add the shrimps and some freshly ground black pepper. Stir gently and then cook for 10 minutes, stirring now and then. Spoon into one dish or small individual ramekins, covering the shrimps with the seasoned butter. They will keep for two weeks in the refrigerator.

(The Vogue Summer Cookbook)

Leith's caterers are now in charge of the restaurants at Glyndebourne for those who wish to play safe with the weather. For inveterate and wealthy picnickers the various options come at a cost of around £58 per head with a half bottle of champagne per couple or £48.50 with white wine plus a variety of possible luxury supplements. These days, if it is wet, there are tents available for sheltering picnickers, although it does rather take the edge off things nonetheless.

If it is true that £1 in 1907 is equivalent to about £85 a century later, Leith's champagne menu, without supplements, is only slightly more expensive than the flat rate of £8..14 shillings and threepence for a hamper for 12, 'suitable for Races, Picnics, Regattas &c', from the Army & Navy Stores in 1907. The 1907 version is, however, a good deal more generous with the drink. It contained 'Boiled Salmon or Lobsters, Pigeon Pie, Roast Fowls, Ham, Rolled Tongue, Salad and Dressing, Mayonnaise Sauce, Bread, Rolls, Butter, Cheese, Cake, Pastry & Condiments' then a bottle of Achille Morat Champagne per head plus 2 bottles of Sherry, 4 of Claret and 1 of Whisky or Brandy'. Linen, plate, glass, cutlery are all included.

Picnic Crumbs

Starters

Asparagus vinaigrette **V**

Smoked salmon and caper berries

Goat's cheese panacotta

Tian of crayfish tails, apple frisée with roast garlic aioli
(Supplement of £4.50)

Chicken liver parfait and quince jelly

Ham terrine with mustard pickle

Cèpe & Taleggio tart **V**

Main Courses

Rare fillet of beef with horseradish sauce

Whole lobster salad **(Supplement of £9.50)**

Poached Scottish salmon fillets with lemon and black pepper

Gressingham duck, sesame seed, mange tout salad & citrus dressing

Trout and pear stack with rocket, watercress and endive

Tomato & spinach celeriac roulade **V**

Puddings & Cheese

English strawberries and cream

Tropical fruit salad **V**

Summer pudding

Chocolate truffe

Lemon tart with crème fraîche

Selection of British cheese **V**

Coffee & Chocolates

PORTER SERVICE

Porter Service for parties of up to 8 persons (Supplement of £25.00)

Above 8 persons - supplement per extra cover (Supplement of £4.00)

FURNITURE

Picnic tables (Supplement of £15.00)

Picnic chairs (Supplement of £6.00)

The best known predecessors of contemporary society picnic dinners, not to mention expensive catering arrangements, are the suppers and refreshments once to be had in the Vauxhall Pleasure Gardens. At their peak during the late 17th and 18th centuries the Gardens were the place to see and be seen although much of the entertainment available was a good deal bawdier than that provided at Glyndebourne. There were over a hundred decorated supper boxes, with seating for six to eight people, in which very small quantities of food were offered at considerable cost. A dish of wafer thin ham cost one shilling and it was said that the Vauxhall carver could cover the whole Gardens with a single joint. By 1817 a minute portion of ham with two chickens cost 11 shillings, biscuits and cheese cakes another 4s..6d and a quart of arrack, 7s. The wines were reputedly excellent and the arrack, made from rum and grains of the medicinal benjamin flower, famously intoxicating.*

'These Flowers are, without doubt, the most essential Part of the Benjamin, whose principal Virtues are as well to subtilize bad Humours and expel them through the Pores of the Skin, as to loosen and expel the thick and viscous by the ordinary Ways, chiefly those of the Breast and Lungs: Dose from three Grains to ten in any proper Liquor. They are profitable in vehement Catarrhs, Coughs, Colds, Asthma's, and Obstructions of the Lungs; procure Sweat excellently in venereal Cases, given in a Decoction of Guajacum, and fortify a weak Stomach.'

(Pierre Pomet, *A Complete History of Druggs* 1709)

---

* The benjamin bush, otherwise known as feverbush or spice bush, provided a herbal remedy for colds, dysentery and intestinal parasites and is still used today in Chinese medicine.

An Apophlegmatic Lohoch

Take Syrup of Hyssop 2 ounces and a half; Oil of sweet Almonds 1 ounce; Oil of Anniseed 2 drops; Tincture of Myrrh 1 dram; powder'd Orris root 4 scruples; Flower of Benjamin half a scruple; Tobacco 4 grains, mix.

By pricking the Parts, drawing the limpid Saliva, inciding thick Phlegm exonerating the Glands, and lubricating the Passages. It brings viscid Phlegm up out of the Throat, and is useful whensoever the Uvula, Parotides, and internal Parts of the Gula are swell'd, and oppress'd with mucous Filth: And when the Secretion is to be provok'd, and a failing Cough to be recover'd.

(Fuller, Pharmacopoeia Extemporanea)

Taking your own dinner or at least a hand in the cooking of it may have made for a more generous dinner than that provided by the carver but the diarist Horace Walpole makes it sound a somewhat haphazard affair.

> 'At last we assembled in our booth, Lady Caroline in the front, with the visor of her hat erect, and looking gloriously jolly and handsome. She had fetched my brother Orford from the next box, where he was enjoying himself with his petite partie, to help us to mince chickens. We minced seven chickens into a china dish, which Lady Caroline stewed over a lamp with three pats of butter and a flagon of water, stirring and rattling, and laughing, and we every minute expecting to have the dish fly about our ears. She brought Betty, the fruit-girl, with hampers of strawberries and cherries from Roger's, and made her wait upon us, and then made her sup by us at a little table.'
>
> (Horace Walpole, *Letters, Vol. II*)

In *The Citizen of the World,* Oliver Goldsmith's Chinese philosopher is invited to the Gardens with friends where: 'The widow found the supper excellent, but Mrs Tibbs thought everything detestable: "Come, come, my dear," cries the husband, by way of consolation, " to be sure we can't find such dressing here as we have at Lord Crump's or Lady Crimp's; but for Vauxhall dressing it is pretty good: it is not their victuals indeed I find fault with, but their wine; "their wine," cries he, drinking off a glass, "indeed is most abominable"'.

The Gardens finally closed in 1859 but by 1821 Eden Pierce was describing the 'refreshments to be of the best quality, and supplied upon moderate terms', a transformation that may have led to the bankruptcy of the owner in 1839.

> 'Now is the cheerful white-covered table set, and decked with polished utensils. The juicy fruits of the hot-house, hyacinthine Xeres in crystal cups, and champagne covered with thick mist, from the ice, await the guests.'
>
> (Pückler-Muskau, *Tours in England*)

As roads and coaches improved during the 18th century, society increasingly decamped to the great country houses for entertainments that whisked them from the ballrooms, down sweeping stone staircases and out into landscaped gardens and parks, ornamented with follies, grottoes and temples. Those at Eaton Hall, Loelia Westminster's sometime home, did not impress the traveller and garden designer Prince Hermann von Pückler-Muskau on a visit in the 1830s. 'A number of 'affreux' little Gothic temples, deface the pleasure-ground, which has, moreover, no fine trees: the soil is not very favourable, and the whole seems laid out in comparatively recent times. The country is rather pretty, though not picturesque, and too flat.'

A new interest in country life and rustic living among the upper classes encouraged the inclusion of estate workers and locals in outdoor entertainment and feasting on a spectacular scale. The 'peasants' were not, it seems, always present solely for their own pleasure.

> 'Yesterday, the wedding day of the Duchess of St. A, was celebrated by a very pleasant rural fete at her villa. In the middle of the bowling-green was a Maypole decorated with garlands and ribands, and gaily-dressed peasants in the old English costume danced around it. The company wandered about in

the house and garden as they liked; many shot with bows and arrows; others danced under tents, swung, or played all sorts of games, or wandered in the shade of thick shrubberies; till at five o'clock a few blasts of a trumpet announced a splendid breakfast, at which all the delicacies and costly viands that luxury could furnish, were served in the greatest profusion.'

The ice cream named in honour of Pückler-Muskau, Fürst Puckler Eis, is a form of Neapolitan which those with a sweet tooth and a taste for colour may enjoy. The original was probably more of a layered iced dessert than the multi-coloured ice cream which is traditionally served sliced, with each slice coated in chocolate sauce and arranged on a plate garnished with whipped cream.

The Review of the Hertfordshire Volunteers and Militia at Hatfield House, home of the Earls of Salisbury, in 1800 was a stupendous feat of conspicuous consumption, attended by the temporarily sane King George III, and other members of the royal family. Estate entertainments to celebrate comings of age or birthdays of landowners or their heirs have continued on great estates to the present day although on a reducing scale in the last hundred years or so.

At Hatfield 25 tables of 25 were set outside the house with one bottle of port per two people; butts of ale and small beer placed 'in different directions' and reserves of wine in case of need. 'The quantity drunk that day in the Park, Tents and House, exceeded 1300 bottles of wine, of various sorts' while some idea of the food is suggested by the list which was 'part of it' and included; 120 pieces of boiled beef; 104 quarters of lamb; 96 pieces of roast beef; 110 joints of veal; 70 hams; 60 meat pies &c; 70 tongues.

> 'In the afternoon of the next day, the remnants were distributed to nearly one thousand persons, exclusive of joints which were clandestinely carried off the evening before.'

The King and the Royal Family had retired indoors to a dinner served in two courses that included:

Voulouvan aux canuffes; Haunch of venison; Grenades de Veau; Pâté de macaroni; Gateau de Savoie; Corbeille de patisserie; Goose roti; Crayfish; and Orange jelly. There was a side table of cold meats, and desert, chiefly of 'forced fruits and ices'. 'Their Majesties after dinner drank coffee and tea in the library', of which one imagines they were much in need. (*Narrative of the Preparations at Hatfield House for the Review of the Volunteer Corps and Militia, 13th June 1800*)

Provisions

'Certain articles which can now be purchased in tins and bottles are so perfectly done that – granted a good cook – it is absolutely impossible to tell the difference between them and fresh. To mention a few at random we would say mushrooms, white currants, raspberries (the Café Grand, Karachi, have some very excellent raspberries in tins which have the great merit of each raspberry being whole), celery, larks in foie gras and strawberries in brandy. None of these can be produced fresh in Sind and therefore if one desires any of them to complete a recherché dinner, it is necessary to obtain them in tins or bottles. Any of the last mentioned items can be obtained from the Army and Navy Stores, London, or Harrods and if ordered direct, are very cheap even including freight and customs duty.'

(*CC Lewis, Culinary Notes for Sind,* quoted in *Curries and Bugles,*
Jennifer Brennan)

'There is a creature something like a whale, for he lives in the cold northern waters as whales often do, and something like an elephant, for he has two ivory tusks, one of which grows long and curved and handsome. He is called a narwhal, and although fewer men have tasted him than have tasted either whale or elephant, his skin is reported to be delicious, crisp as celery and tasting of nuts and mushroom – and looking like half-inch thick linoleum, which for me at least would prove an esthetic handicap.'

(M. F. K. Fisher)

There are plenty of travellers' and cooks' accounts in this book that include recommendations as to fitting provisions for a particular occasion or journey; that important business is the prelude to most accounts of travelling food and picnics. In Hong Kong forgetting the ice or the lemons, the unfailing necessities of boating picnics, may have been grounds for divorce but not a matter of life and death. For expeditions to extreme destinations like Everest and Antarctica, mistakes or omissions in provisioning could tip the balance, already slight enough, between success or failure and the loss of life against which gung ho fortitude, tweed plus fours and a good dose of British phlegm was hollow insurance. The deaths of all members of Sir John Franklin's famously failed expedition to find the North West Passage in 1845 has been in part at least attributed to contaminated tinned foods in the earliest days of the tinning process, trichinosis from infested polar bear meat and straightforward starvation that may or may not have resulted in cases of cannibalism. The provisions, perishables and preserves of picnic and travel food and the requirements for cooking and eating it are worth close attention.

The apparently amateur nature of Captain Scott's 1901-1904 'Discovery Expedition' to Antarctica did not preclude considerable research into suitable rations that included advice from Fridtjof Nansen, the Norwegian Arctic explorer. We are now aware that Scott was a good deal more professional in his preparations than suited the idea of the British hero at the time. In a letter to Sir Clements Markham, President of the Royal Geographic Society and major supporter of the National Antarctic Expedition, Nansen recommends the Stavanger Preserving Company, now a museum, as providers of 'tinned mackerel', 'excellent, the very best food we had aboard' and *fiskefarce*, 'something we never got tired of eating'.

This recipe comes from *For Danish Appetites:*

Fiskefars (Fish forcemeat)

1lb lean white fish; 4 tablespoons potato; 3 tablespoons melted butter; 2 tbsp each flour and cornflour; 1 teaspoon salt; pepper; 1 egg well beaten; 1/2c. Milk

Grind fish, using the fine blade on your grinder, or whirl in a blender, a little at a time, until all is smooth. Add butter, flour and cornstarch. Add seasoning to taste, and beaten egg. Mix very well, using an electric mixer. Gradually add milk, beating constantly, until absorbed. This mixture can either be fried in spoonfuls or baked as fiskebudding : butter a 1 quart mould and sprinkle with breadcrumbs. Add the fiskefars. Set mould in a pan of hot water and bake in oven 325° for 1 hour.

This makes 4 servings.

Scott himself was closely involved with the proper provisioning of the expedition, following up an order for 1,000 pounds of Cartridge Pemmican to the American Compressed Food Co. in Passaic, New Jersey on 23rd April, 1901, with another letter on 25th asking for only 500lbs to be delivered since:

> It has been pointed out that your pemmican contains 43% only of Ox Lard. This is not serious, but compared with other pemmicans, the nutritive value is, I regret to say, not satisfactory.

In fact, as Nansen may well have pointed out, the expedition diet would have been improved and more likely to stave off the scurvy suffered by its members with less preserved and more of the fresh meat available from seals, penguins, and, as they turned out to be of little use to the British with no idea how to use them in their sledges, their dogs. Supplies, including black and white pepper and mustard, rum, butter, lime juice, tea and chocolate foods, were inspected by the Government Laboratory. This may have been a sensible precaution given reports showing that one pemmican sample 'contained pieces of steel, probably from the machinery with which prepared, weighing rather more than half an ounce'. The testing of all tins was essential for the importance of them being 'free from taint'.

The laboratory report finds 'somatose' unsuitable, 'said to be processed from beef but is tasteless and contains no characteristic substance it is impossible to trace its precise origin.' The description of somatose in *The Wide Encyclopedia of Cookery. An Encyclopedic Handbook for the Homemaker covering Foods and Beverages-their Purchase, Preparation, and Service* adds further detail: 'Beef Somatose is a commercial product used in invalid diets, somatose is a granular predigested meat powder which contains a large amount of albumin and is free of peptones. It has a yellowish color and a faint taste and odor. Dissolved in water it forms a light yellow solution having almost no taste or odor.' Nutritious or not, it sounds too horrible for words.

The 'Food list for three years with quantities and costs for 40 men' included:

3,000 lbs roast beef
750 lbs roast kidney
750 lbs rabbit
250 lbs tripe and onions
16,000 Cabin biscuits
25,000 Extra Navy (biscuits)

'Medical comforts' of:
25 gallons each of brandy and whisky
36 gallons of sherry
25 gallons of virol
75 gallons of Devonshire cream
150 gallons each of chicken and mutton broth
576 of Nestlés and Viking milk

Assorted sauces, including wild cherry, perhaps to accompany the tinned duck; 200lbs of egg powder, 800 gallons of rum to be dispensed 2 ounces daily per man (the standard Navy ration from 1850-1970), 1,800lbs tobacco (1lb monthly), 3,500lbs cheddar.

On the 7th May 1900, Clements Markham's *Report to Hygiene Committee* points out that 'preserved potatoes are not good but it is said that if frozen potatoes are plunged at once into boiling water without previous thawing, they are found to be perfectly good as regards taste. This deserves consideration'

He also suggests the carrying of livestock in large enough quantities to be killed and frozen 'as soon as the temperature is low enough, to which might perhaps be added seal and penguin flesh sufficient to last through a winter'.

The invoice from 'Maconochie Bros. Ltd, Manufacturers of jams, pickles, sauces, soups, preserved fish & meats of all kinds' of July 6th 1901 comes to £1,437.. 5 shillings and 7 pence.

Harrods Stores Ltd were the suppliers for the British National Antarctic Expedition relief ship *Morning*, providing, with barrels of salt beef; the Plasmon (homogenised) beef; tins of jugged hare and partridges; a large supply of tinned vegetables; preserved and dried fruits; various tinned fish, halibut, salmon, gurnet, soles; pickles and chutneys and 200 ¼ lb tins of curry powder plus other spices. It sounds just what you would expect in an old fashioned country house larder but on a larger scale. I remember tinned ham and others which never could live up to the labels on the tin however grand their retailer. It must be said that by and large tins originating in France, whether of foie gras, coq au vin or petit pois, more usually exceeded anticipation. Good or bad, all those tins sat higgledy piggledy on mid-20th century larder shelves awaiting the nuclear winter and rusting gently until their lids popped, a clearer indication of inedibility than any sell by date.

Harrods also provided the wherewithal for serving all this food; sauce tureens and ladles; egg cups and a desert set; fish carvers and toast racks; napkins, oven cloths and fancy dinner mats; cut table bottles and   24

has been the equivalent of the total input of a normal person. It is exactly as though a normal person had eaten nothing, I repeat nothing, all this time. After several weeks they would get weak and desperately hungry. In fact they would starve. We are slowly starving".

This, of course, was a godsend for Mike's research work. After sixty days of watching Mike divide our daily ration in two and hand me one vitamin tablet, four small-size milk chocolate bars, eight sheets of loo paper (inedible) and one crunchy flapjack, I began to nurse horrible suspicions that he was handing me the smaller of the flapjacks every day. This irked me as I grew more ravenous until, on the sixty-first day, I suggested that we take turns to choose the daily flapjacks. Mike agreed readily enough.'

When Jeffa Murray, the first female helicopter pilot to fly solo round the world, followed up in 2003 by an attempt to fly from pole to pole, she was also going to meet her husband, Simon, in Antarctica on his quest to become the oldest man to walk to the South Pole beside the explorer Pen Hadow. Weight implications required both husband and wife to survive largely on dehydrated food but communication afforded by satellite phone allowed Simon to order up more solid supplies for helicopter delivery to the Pole – bacon, eggs, butter and a frying pan.

Isabella Bird, the Victorian traveller who, except when travelling, suffered ill health all her life, especially during her mid-life six years marriage to Edinburgh doctor John Bishop, had a great deal to say on all aspects of the countries she visited. The 'Food Question' for her travels in Japan gets its fair share of acerbic comment and she deals with it entirely to her own satisfaction. One gets the feeling from her letters to her sister that her diet during her tour may indeed have consisted largely of tea and rice enlivened presumably with her meagre personal supplies and the occasional 'fowl of much experience'.

'If I accepted much of the advice given to me, as to taking tinned meats and soups, claret, and a Japanese maid, I should need a train of at least six pack-horses. 'The "Food Question" is said to be the most important one for all travellers, and it is discussed continually with startling earnestness, not alone as regards my tour. However apathetic people are on other subjects, the mere mention of this one rouses them into interest. All have suffered or may suffer, and every one wishes to impart his own experience or to learn from that of others. Foreign ministers, professors, missionaries, merchants - all discuss it with becoming gravity as a question of life and death, which by many it is supposed to be. The fact is that, except at a few hotels in popular resorts which are got up for foreigners, bread, butter, milk, meat, poultry, coffee, wine, and beer, are unattainable, that fresh fish is rare, and that unless one can live on rice, tea, and eggs, with the addition now and then of some tasteless fresh vegetables, food must be taken, as the fishy and vegetable abominations known as "Japanese food" can only be swallowed and digested by a few, and that after long practice.

'The "Food Question" has been solved by a modified rejection of all advice! I have only brought a small supply of Liebig's extract of meat, 4 lbs. of raisins, some chocolate, both for eating and drinking, and some brandy in case of need. 'When we stopped at wayside tea-houses the runners bathed their feet, rinsed their mouths, and ate rice, pickles, salt fish, and "broth of abominable things", after which they smoked their tiny pipes, which give them three whiffs for each filling. As soon as I got out at any of these, one smiling girl brought me the tabako-bon, a square wood or lacquer tray, with a china or bamboo charcoal-holder and ash-pot upon it, and another presented me with a zen, a small lacquer table about six inches high, with a tiny teapot with a hollow handle at right angles with the spout, holding about an English tea-cupful, and two cups without handles or saucers, with a capacity of from ten to twenty thimblefuls each. The hot water is merely allowed to rest a minute on the tea-leaves, and the infusion is a clear straw-coloured liquid with a delicious aroma and flavour, grateful and refreshing at all times. If Japanese tea "stands," it acquires a coarse bitterness and an unwholesome astringency. Milk and sugar are not used. A clean-looking wooden or lacquer pail with a lid is kept in all tea-houses, and though hot rice, except to order, is only ready three times daily, the pail always contains cold rice, and the coolies heat it by pouring hot tea over it. As you eat, a tea-house girl, with this pail beside her, squats on the floor in front of you, and fills your rice bowl till you say, "Hold, enough!" On this road it is expected that you leave three or four sen on the tea-tray for a rest of an hour or two and tea.' (*Unbeaten Tracks in Japan, An Account of Travels in the Interior including Visits to the Aborigines of Yezo and the Shrine of Nikko*)

The 'food question' arises again in more comic form in *Three Men in a Boat*, the matter of travelling with cheese being particularly vexatious.

'For other breakfast things, George suggested eggs and bacon, which were easy to cook, cold meat, tea, bread and butter, and jam. For lunch, he said, we could have biscuits, cold meat, bread and butter, and jam - but NO CHEESE. Cheese, like oil, makes too much of itself. It wants the whole boat to itself. It goes through the hamper, and gives a cheesy flavour to everything else there. You can't tell whether you are eating apple-pie or German sausage, or strawberries and cream. It all seems cheese. There is too much odour about cheese.

I remember a friend of mine, buying a couple of cheeses at Liverpool. Splendid cheeses they were, ripe and mellow, and with a two hundred horse-power scent about them that might have been warranted to carry three miles, and knock a man over at two hundred yards.

Fond as I am of cheese, therefore, I hold that George was right in declining to take any.

"We shan't want any tea," said George (Harris's face fell at this); "but we'll have a good round, square, slap-up meal at seven - dinner, tea, and supper combined."

Harris grew more cheerful. George suggested meat and fruit pies, cold meat, tomatoes, fruit, and green stuff. For drink, we took some wonderful sticky concoction of Harris's, which you mixed with water and called lemonade, plenty of tea, and a bottle of whisky, in case, as George said, we got upset.

(Jerome K Jerome *Three Men in a Boat*)

Fynes Morrison's *Itinerary* gives a clear picture of the travel food of the late 16th century, which, in the Mediterranean at least, doesn't sound too bad at all, especially given the liberal quantities of wine he lists. For our enjoyment he also gives brief sketches of some of his fellow travellers and consumers.

'This Fleming was a fat man, borne to consume victuals, & he had now spent in his journey to Venice thirty pound sterling, and here for his journey to Jerusalem had already put into the ship full Hogs-heads of Wine, and store of all victuals, when suddenly he changed his minde, for feare of a great Rhume wherewith he was troubled, or being discouraged with the difficulty of the journey, and would needs returne to Emden, with purpose (if hee were to be believed) to returne the next Spring to some place neere Jerusalem, in an English ship, which he thought more commodious. He professed, that he had put much money out upon his returne, and since hee was old, and very sickly, and after so long a journey, and so much money spent, would needes returne home, I cannot thinke that he ever undertooke this journey againe.'

The *Itinerary* describes in careful detail the fresh food supplied by his ship's Master for the first few days out of port en route from Cyprus to Joppa (Jaffa), that was followed by hard 'bisket', salt or pickled fish for fasting days, 'oyle in stead of butter, nuts, fruit, cheese and like things'. Fynes and his brother took emergency rations of their own of dried fruit, 'very white bisket' and naturally 'some flaggons of rich wine', not neglecting ginger and nutmeg 'to comfort our stomackes in case of weakness' and other remedies for chills and agues 'some cooling sirops, and some pounds of sugar, and some laxative medicines'. Such precautions were well taken in the face of a barrel of wine that 'fretted our very intrals' for a cost of 'one Zechine, and foure soldi of Venice, and two Turkish aspers'.

A century and a half or so later, the novelist Tobias Smollett, wrote his *Travels through France and Italy*. His views on the importance of carrying his own food and supplies in order to avoid the expense and dubious quality of the food available at the wayside auberge are a foretaste of those later opinions of Mrs Jekyll and Sir Francis Colchester Wemyss in the first half of the 20th century. Smollet was a curious enough traveller but one has a sense that he was the sort who would rather have observed what foreigners ate than eat it himself; he invariably sounds surprised when he finds something that he likes. In another era he would definitely have carried his own cornflakes on trips abroad, and a pot of Marmite.

> 'For my part, I hate the French cookery, and abominate garlic, with which all their ragouts in this part of the country are highly seasoned: we therefore formed a different plan of living upon the road. Before we left Paris, we laid in a stock of tea, chocolate, cured neats' tongues, and saucissons, or Bologna sausages, both of which we found in great perfection in that capital, where, indeed, there are excellent provisions of all sorts. About ten in the morning we stopped to breakfast at some auberge, where we always found bread, butter, and milk. In the mean time, we ordered a poulard or two to be roasted, and these, wrapped in a napkin, were put into the boot of the coach, together with bread, wine, and water. About two or three in the afternoon, while the horses were changing, we laid a cloth upon our knees, and producing our store, with a few earthen plates,discussed our short meal without further ceremony. This was followed by a dessert of grapes and other fruit, which we had also provided. I must own I found these transient refreshments much more agreeable than any regular meal I ate upon the road.'

Disasters, Discomforts and Emergency Rations

'While, however, even the most enthusiastic adherents of the picnic will scarcely deny that the sunny hours of preparation that herald the inevitable downpour when you set out, are the most enjoyable, or that it is often more pleasurable in reality to think of a picnic, while steadfastly remaining in your own dining room, than to attend one, nevertheless the idea is undoubtedly enticing, calls you away from worries, from the cares and dust of cities.'

(Osbert Sitwell, *Picnics and Pavilions*)

Claudia Roden quotes Georgina Battiscombe in *English Picnics* (1951) saying the English picnicker is something of a stoic in the face of our unreliable climate, going on to add that an uncomfortable picnic may still have the edge over the food available in British hotels and restaurants. While this may sometimes be the case, there remain all sorts of good reasons for picnics, not least economic. Roden suggests a certain masochistic delight taken by the British picnicker in the anticipation of disaster. Stories of disaster lose nothing in the telling but for those like me who find little pleasure before, during, or after the event, in a cold, wet picnic, or the clouds of midges descending to clear a Scottish beach in record time, some are more amusing than others. There are situations too that require extreme improvisation and emergency rations and are a good deal more life-threatening than such small outdoor dramas or those that enliven Victorian diaries like those of Maud Berkeley.

Picnic Crumbs

Adapted by Flora Fraser, the *Diaries of Maud Berkeley* are jauntily illustrated with her drawings and watercolours and are packed with picnics where minor disaster adds to the entertainment, at least after the event. The picnickers are always accompanied by 'that invaluable aid to every picnic – an umbrella'. Until her marriage, Maud lived on the Isle of Wight, definitely picnic territory but prey to the usual vagaries of the British climate. A 'lovely picnic' on a July sketching excursion with friends had a less satisfactory encore:

> 'Very cold. Heard from Mrs Hatchet, whom we met on the Prom as we were setting out, that there was snow at Portsmouth. Decided in favour of nearby Culver Cliffs for a picnic spot, instead of going further afield. Would never have thought it was high summer. Sat on the sands and shivered our way through cups of tea and toast grilled ineffectually on a pile of sticks. I wore my new hat with the veil, which rather incommoded my attempts to eat and drink.'

On another occasion, 'Mollie Boucher brought a teapot which leaked through the spout, so we were not very adequately served. It was so cold, that, after on an hour or so, we retreated back to Sandown.'

A beach picnic today may be a very different sort of disaster. Digby Anderson describes a family on the beach in *The English at Table* which is at best depressing. 'They had been eating intermittently through the morning and were to continue eating throughout the afternoon' a menu of pizza; bacon and cheese puffs, 'soggy chips covered with tomato ketchup – hamburgers with more ketchup'; 'industrial ice creams with brightly coloured things in them'. Everything was eaten with the fingers except the chips, shovelled into greedy mouths in a 'refined' way with wooden forks. There were bars of chocolate, fizzy drinks and lager for grownups. After 'each instalment of food, one member of the fractured family dutifully took a pile of the polystyrene dishes to throw away in the litter bin. A casual inspection revealed that the dishes had enough chips and ketchup still on them to feed Somalia.'

A bizarre 18th century prank, carefully contrived to shock him to the core, became an unusual picnic disaster for the local vicar at West Wycombe Park, the seat of Sir Francis Dashwood, Postmaster General and founder of the Medmenham Abbey Hellfire Club. Invited by the locally popular Sir Francis to bring his Sunday School for a picnic in the newly laid out gardens, the vicar was taken up the tower by his host, better to observe the delightful view. 'To the minister's astonishment a stream of water shot suddenly from the shrubbery and, from the two red-mounted beds, fountains sprayed out white chalky rivers. They were looking down on the naked body of a woman contrived from the contours of the lawn and plants.' The minister fainted clean away. (Phillippa Pullar, *Consuming Passions*)

Victorian heroism was the regular flip side of major disaster, nicely wrapped in mourning ribbons for the chauvinist and sentimental audience at home. Lord Chelmsford's picnic breakfast at Isandlwana in 1879, at the start of the latest imperialist adventure, if not itself a disaster, was the overly relaxed prelude to a catastrophe for the General and his army, albeit with comforting sidelines of heroism and death at Rorke's Drift, in the best Victorian tradition. The whole Zulu war was an ill-conceived land-grab, the battle lost due to the arrogance of British commanders' assumptions of their strength versus that of natives armed with spears. In the end, the Zulu victors suffered most, crushed by the mechanised weight of imperial vengeance until the Zulu kingdom was shattered.

The picnic is described by Commandant Hamilton-Browne, a colonial officer commanding a contingent of African troops and gives the sense of the total unpreparedness of the English command for what was to follow:

> 'I shall never forget the sight of that peaceful picnic. Here were the staff quietly breakfasting and the whole column scattered over the country! Over there the guns unlimbered, over the hills parties of mounted infantry and volunteers looting the scattered kraals for grain for their horses, a company of the 24th one place and another far away.'

> (Ron Lock and Peter Quantrill, *Zulu Victory*)

Picnic Crumbs

The dramas of a boat trip in another part of the Victorian Empire, a year or two earlier are worthy of Jerome K. Jerome's imagination. In *Life in the Mofussil* the author details his life as assistant magistrate and collector in various stations in Bengal and includes an uncomfortable boat trip en route between Muzufferpore, now Muzaffarpur, in Bihar, to Calcutta.

'We had stuck on a sand bank, covered with only about half a foot of water. Oars and poles were at once put in requisition to shove us off; but the wind drove us on, and though Melville and I worked as hard as the rest, all our efforts were of no use, and we became convinced that we must stick where we were until the wind should moderate. My solar topee (pith hat) was whirled away during the struggle, but that was the only result. As the day passed on, about 6 a.m., I began to feel hungry, and would have given a good deal for a hot cup of coffee and a piece of toast. We looked at our leg of lamb, or rather the small remnant. There was no bread left, and we each had a bit of meat and a sweet biscuit, not a nice mixture, our drink being drawn from the holy Ganges, which trouble-some river we both cursed from the bottom of our hearts.

About midday we felt hungry, and again turned our attention to the remnant of our leg of lamb. To our dismay it had turned green. The damp and muggy heat combined had caused this. With many misgivings we committed it to the stream, to be digested by some river turtle or alligator, and satiated our present pangs with a few sweet biscuits each. Evening came on, but with no change, and we were content to dine off a handful of dry rice, given us by the boatmen; for the wind and rain was such that they could not even attempt to light a fire in our exposed situation.

About ten, a steamer passed us, a long way off; but without taking any notice of our signal of distress, viz., a pair of trousers, belonging to Melville, hauled up the mast. We used these in order to show the steamer people that Europeans were on our country boat. We anathematized this vessel pretty well;

but two hours afterwards, another passed us with the same result, and then our indignation knew no bounds. I mentally composed a tremendous letter to the *Englishman* newspaper on the inhuman conduct of river steamer captains, which, as may be supposed, was never committed to writing. Probably we were not seen, and if we were, I doubt if they could have helped us without considerable risk; for it seemed we had got on a long strip of shallow, to which they were obliged to give a wide berth, and down the side of this a tremendous current was running; and had they stopped near, they would probably have been stranded like ourselves. For all this we were not prepared to make allowances at the time; and to add to our discomfort, the bottom of the boat being now pretty well waterlogged, the rats began to make their appearance in our neighbourhood, and to climb about the thatch roof. We consoled ourselves with the reflection that they would not find much to eat, "Unless it should be our own unhappy persons," I added, with a forced smile; but Melville suggested that it might be the other way, and we should eat them.

(Life in the Mofussil, Or the Civilian in Lower Bengal)

According to Calvin W. Schwabe in *Unmentionable Food*, 'Brown Rats and roof rats were eaten openly on a large scale in Paris when the city was under siege during the Franco-Prussian War. Observers likened their taste to both partridge and pork.' Not the only time in history the detested rodents provided sustenance although we are more likely these days to think of rat eating only in the context of a Blackadder joke. In the China of Marco Polo's time, rat was known as 'household deer' (Reay Tannahill, *Food in History*) and a simple recipe for rat, as eaten in certain regions of France, is included in the *Larousse Gastronomique*.

'The flesh of well-nourished rats can be, it seems of good quality, but sometimes with a musky taste. Rats nourished in the wine stores of the Gironde were at one time highly esteemed by the coopers, who grilled them, after having cleaned out and skinned them, on a fire of broken barrels, and seasoned them with a little oil and plenty of shallot. This dish which was then called Cooper's Entrecôte, would be the origin of the Entrecôte à la bordelaise.'

During the 1870 siege of Paris, Choron, the chef at the famous Voisin restaurant, created a menu to celebrate Christmas, the 99th day of the siege, that legend has it included elephant soup made from Castor and Pollux, the two elephants of the zoo; stuffed donkey head, roasted camel, kangaroo stew, rack of bear, leg of wolf, cat garnished with rats, and antelope pie. Not that unusual dishes were entirely alien to the restaurant, saddle of spaniel being served earlier as a meat course. M.F.K. Fisher writes of eating shrimp the first time as an equal test to dishes we find positively barbaric.

'I must eat at least one shrimp, and then die or be sick.' But once tasted things changed so the shrimps, lobsters and all their armoured relations became some 'of the sweetest things in this world to put between my teeth.'

In the middle of Queen Victoria's reign, poor weather, bad harvests and lack of care for the labouring classes affected the rural poor in Britain no less than in more distant parts of her fabulous Empire. At the centre of it all in London, starvation stalked the streets as closely as it did in besieged Paris. *Oliver Twist* was merely an individualised portrait that described the lives of starving children all over the city, where families, with no space, facilities or fuel for cooking in slum tenements, were eating whatever they could afford, scrounge or steal from the streets of the capital. Children in particular suffered the consequences of malnutrition with rickets, tuberculosis and other diseases exacerbated by vitamin deficiency, even the seafarers' scourge, scurvy, came ashore to claim its share of victims. The cheapest food on the streets, other than discarded eel heads, were loaves of bread, or baked potatoes bought from vendors and used to warm frozen hands for as long as possible before eating.

Brewis is poor food for the poor; a crust of bread upon which boiling water is poured, then drained, flavoured with salt and pepper if available and to be eaten with a spoon. Florence White includes a recipe from the 1840s in her collection of traditional foods, *Good Things in England*; it is uncomfortable to imagine the circumstances under which this would be good. Fish became cheap food as the railways brought ever greater supplies from the coast; a bit of fried fish cost a penny; shellfish, kippers and sprats were sold from street barrows. Eels, pea soup, pickled herrings, baked apples, sheep's trotters and muffins were staple street food; penny pies, often made of bad meat disguised with treacle and the strong seasoning that people expected. Sweeney Todd's favourite economy cuts may or may not have been pure fiction. Children bought sweets coloured with arsenic, mercury and lead and the first immigrant Italian ice cream makers sold 'penny licks', often made with dirty milk, cornstarch and lurid colourings.

Worst of all, according to the English women's *Domestic Magazine,* published and edited by Samuel and Isabella Beeton, was the spectacle of boys scouring discarded animal hides by the markets round London Bridge for any piece of meat still adhering to the skin. 'This was poverty's larder – crawling with knife wielding boys "hunting about the hides and flapping them over to get at their fleshy side", swooping down on a tag of meat "like a carrion crow on a worm".' (Kate Coquhoun, *Taste*)

Florence White's collection has an 1870s recipe for eel pie. It may use Thames eels but it sounds like middle class food, the sort of thing enjoyed alfresco by day trippers and the members of the Twickenham Rowing Club on Eel Pie Island, not the cheap food being sold from a stall in the East End of London.

Thames Eel Pie

'Puff pastry; Thames eels 2; hard-boiled eggs; shallots 2 small ones; butter ½oz.; parsley a small faggot chopped; nutmeg; pepper; salt; and sherry 2 glasses; water. For the sauce: butter 2oz.; flour 2oz.; lemon the juice of a whole one. For preparation and cooking 1½ to 2 hours all told.

Skin, cleanse and bone two Thames eels. Cut these in pieces. Chop the shallots; pass them in butter for 5 or 6 minutes and then add to them a small faggot of parsley chopped, with nutmeg, pepper, salt, and two glasses of sherry. In the midst of this place the eels, add enough water to cover them, and set them on the fire to boil. When they have boiled up, take out the pieces of eel and keep them hot. Strain the stock in which they were cooked. Melt the butter and add the flour in the usual way for a foundation sauce. Add the strained stock, beat quite smooth, boil up and finish with the juice of a whole lemon. Arrange the pieces of eel, and quarters of hard-boiled eggs in a pie dish. Pour the sauce over it, and when cold, roof the pie with puff pastry. Bake in a hot oven at first, to raise the pastry and then in a cooler one, one hour all told.'

Eels in any form were highly nutritious at least. The Medical Research Council reported in 1928 that 'the body oil in eels (almost 30% of their whole substance) contains not only vitamin D, but almost as much vitamin A as good cod liver oil – a striking confirmation of the medieval notion that eels have high dietetic value'. And a reason for all the ruins and remains of eel stew ponds in the grounds of ancient monasteries and manors. Eels apparently went out of fashion because it was believed that they had to be skinned alive, not an encouraging idea. I wish we had known as children that eels could be killed instantly by 'piercing the spinal marrow, close to the back part of the skull' – we had usually cut them into several pieces before all motion ceased and they held none of the appeal of other, easier, wild food.

The vinegary cockles, mussels, winkles and whelks of traditional London street stalls are the same as we gathered fresh on the summer beaches of childhood holidays, besides buckets of shrimps collected in nets with a wooden board to push through the sandy bottom of the shallows. Arabella Boxer remembers a friend's story of her nanny eating winkles raw with her hat pin on the beach at Ramsgate before World War 1. Our nanny, at a later date, brought them home to be boiled and then eaten with a large nappy pin. I don't remember that we acquired the taste and I'm none too sure that Nanny really liked them either, they looked too horrible with their lids like blackened finger nails but I can't imagine why we should think them much worse than escargots if we swapped the vinegar for butter and garlic. Cockles are best eaten raw, although they are chewy; mussels, we still gather from the rocks in Scotland on days when we feel energetic enough to scrub them clean or just boil them up with onion, wine and garlic, strain the sauce of grit and pick out the flesh, discarding shells and beards.

Undoubtedly, as children we were spoilt for improvised food and what we would then have seen as emergency rations. A kitchen garden full of ripening peas, pears and peaches in green-houses; the smell of strawberry patches and fruit hidden under leaves; the occasional wasp sting among the raspberry canes and the alien looking hairy gooseberries, rarely perfect and sweet enough to eat raw. Beyond the immediate confines of home, autumn orchards of apples, wild raspberries in the woods and miles of hedgerows full of blackberries, nuts and the bitter sloes and damsons used to make deep red fruit gins and vodkas.

This is instant food for innocents. With all the survival experts we now have on our televisions, let alone the repellent bush dishes served up for contestants in competitive jungle reality programmes, we now know that we can survive anywhere on the occasional stick insect or a small termite nest. We can discover from a whole history of adventure and exploration on sea and land the dos and don'ts of provisioning and staying alive but accidents happen and there are still places in our smaller, better known world, where the best laid plans may fail with no emergency rations to fall back on.

The Donner Party were a disparate group of 81 mid-western farmers and businessmen travelling from Wyoming during the winter of 1846-47 to resettle in California. They paid a high price for badly underestimating the rigours and requirements of the journey; of the original number, 48 survived from groups either left in camp or attempting to keep going and get help. After all their animals had been stolen by Indians, killed for food down to the last pet dog and eaten down to the last piece of stewed hide; they resorted to cannibalism of the dead and of two unfortunate Indian guides who became weak and were considered of little enough account to be killed. Some learned to enjoy human flesh more than others; Lewis Keseberg, the sole survivor at the Donner Lake camp, was found with a pot of human soup and was heard to say that flesh of Mrs Tamsen Donner was the best he had ever tasted. He continued to profess a preference for human brains and liver above other meat which may have contributed to the ultimate failure of his hotel and restaurant business in Sacramento.

The Donner Party Cookbook by anthropologist Terry Alan del Bene gives 19th century recipes for buffalo tongue, antelope and elk that would have been eaten to eke out basic supplies of bacon, beans and hard tack. It includes rather tactless recipes for brains and liver but, aside perhaps from Keseberg, the survivors of the journey were appalled by the means of their survival.

The following account from the *California Star* was the sensationalist tabloid and completely untrue version of events:

> A more shocking scene cannot be imagined, than that witnessed by the party of men who went to the relief of the unfortunate emigrants in the California Mountains. The bones of those who had died and been devoured by the miserable ones that still survived were lying around their tents and cabins. Bodies of men, women and children, with half the flesh torn

from them, lay on every side. A woman sat by the body of her husband, who had just died, eating out his tongue; the heart she had already taken out, broiled, and ate! The daughter was seen eating the flesh of the father - the mother that of her children - children that of father and mother. The emaciated, wild, and ghastly appearance of the survivors, added to the horror of the scene. Language cannot describe the awful change that a few weeks of dire suffering had wrought in the minds of these wretched and pitiable beings. Those who but one month before would have shuddered and sickened at the thought of eating human flesh, or of killing their companions and relatives to preserve their own lives, now looked upon the opportunity by these acts afforded them of escaping the most dreadful of deaths, as a providential interference in their behalf. Calculations were coldly made, as they sat gloomily around their gloomy camp fires, for the next and succeeding meals. Various expedients were devised to prevent the dreadful crime of murder, but they finally resolved to kill those who had the least claims to longer existence. Just at this moment, however, as if by Divine interpolation, some of them died, which afforded the rest temporary relief. Some sunk into the arms of death cursing God for their miserable fate, while the last whisperings of others were prayers and songs of praise to the Almighty.

After the first few deaths, nothing but the one all absorbing thought of individual self-preservation prevailed. The fountains of natural affection were dried up. The cords that once vibrated with connubial, parental and filial affection were rent asunder, and each one seemed resolved without regard to the fate of others to escape from the impending calamity. Even the wild hostile mountain Indians, who once visited their camps, pitied them, and instead of pursuing the natural impulse of their hostile feelings to whites, and destroying them as they could easily have done, divided their own scanty supply of food with them.

So changed had the emigrants become that when the party sent out, arrived with food, some of them cast it aside and seemed to prefer the putrid human flesh that still remained. The day before the party arrived, one of the emigrants took a child of about four years of age in bed with him, and devoured the whole before morning; and the next day eat another about the same age before noon.

It is thought that several more of these unfortunate people might have been saved, but for their determination not to leave their property. Some of them who started in, loaded themselves with their money and other effects to such an extent, that they sunk under them and died on the road. According to the best accounts, forty-three died from starvation. They were principally from the neighbourhood of Independence, Missouri.

In 1972 another story of cannibalism and survival in the most extreme circumstances hit the headlines when 16 people survived ten weeks in the Andes after the plane chartered by an Uruguayan amateur rugby team, 45 passengers crashed in heavy snow. 16 people were eventually rescued including Nando Parrrado and Roberto Canessa, the 'expeditionaries', who walked out of the mountains to reach civilisation in Chile. Once the decision had been made to eat human flesh and the compulsion of starvation made it possible to swallow the strips of meat, it remained a hideous task to slice it from bodies well preserved by the cold and all too recognisably those of their friends and colleagues.

'They had, from necessity, come to eat almost every part of the body. Canessa knew that the liver contained the reserve of vitamins; for that reason he ate it himself and encouraged others to do so until it was set aside for the expeditionaries. Having overcome their revulsion against eating the liver, it was easier to move on to the heart, kidneys and intestines. It was less extraordinary for them to do this than it might have been for a European or a North American, because it was common in Uruguay to eat the intestines and the lymphatic glands of a steer at an asado. The sheets of fat which had been cut from the body were dried in the sun until a crust formed, and then they were eaten by everyone. It was a source of energy and, though not as popular as the meat, was outside the rationing, as were the odd pieces of earlier carcasses which had been left around in the snow and could be scavenged by anyone.'

At night, the boys escaped the horrors of their days, the cold and their cramped and filthy quarters in part of the wrecked plane's fuselage by talking, inevitably about food and in turn describing favourite dishes from their former lives.

'Nogueira, before he died, presented them with cream, meringues, and dulce-de-leche, a thick sweet sauce made with milk and sugar, with a taste between that of condensed milk and caramel cream. Harley, as a winter dish, thought of peanuts and dulce-de-leche coated with chocolate, and, in summer, peanuts and dulce-de-leche ice cream. Algorta had no dish which he could cook himself, but he offered the boys the paella his father sometimes made and his uncle's gnocchi. Parrado could promise the barenkis cooked by his Ukrainian grandmother; and for those who did not know what they were he described these little pancakes filled with cheese, ham, and mashed potatoes. Vizintín, who always spent the summer by the sea near the Brazilian border, described a bouillabaisse, and Methol told him that when they returned he would get Vizintín to show him how to make it.'

Eventually discussion of food was banned as too depressing when faced by reality but the dreams continued.

'Carlitos dreamed of an orange suspended in the air above him. On another occasion he dreamed that a flying saucer came and hovered over the plane. Stairs were lowered and a stewardess came out. He asked her for a strawberry milkshake but was given only a glass of water with a strawberry floating on the top. Roy dreamed that he was in a bakery where biscuits were being shovelled out of the oven. He tried to tell the baker that they were up in the Andes but could not make him understand.'

(Piers Paul Read, *Alive: The Story of the Andes Survivors*)

The Andes survivors were all good Roman Catholics from a college run by the Irish Christian Brothers and were assured on their return that their church accepted that anthropophagy in extremis was not a sin. The hooligan behaviour of the first crusaders, ravaging and pillaging their way to the Holy Land was less easily forgiven by the Turks and Saracens whose spies discovered the bodies of the hungry Christians' captives roasting on spits in their kitchens.

Eating enemies is a not entirely rare event throughout history; to eat friends, however dead and even for survival is a different matter entirely. M.F.K. Fisher follows up her first taste of prawns with a 'dangerously disgusting' oyster; but she goes on to say that she ate, thereafter, oysters whenever she could. This included a 'very bad one in Berne' that her husband assured her would prove to be safe provided she did not die within six hours. 'I did not, although the last hour had me waiting with ill-concealed anxiety, my eyes on the clock and one hand lying expectantly upon the bedside bell'.

She later learned from 'no less an authority than Henri Charpentier' that she should have drunk large quantities of rough red wine, the tannic content of which being a well-known antidote to the acid of a 'rotting mollusc'. She regrets she has not had the opportunity to test this cure, not having since been in 'oysterish places'.

In *Consider the Oyster*, Fisher manages to encourage sympathy for the oyster beyond our fondness for its flesh. 'Life is hard, we say. An oyster's life is worse. She lives motionless, soundless, her own cold ugly shape her only dissipation, and if she escapes the menace of duck-slipper-mussel-Black-Drum-leech-sponge-borer-starfish, it is for man to eat, because of man's own hunger.'

School Food

At Hurstpierpoint College in Sussex, on Ascension Day, the whole school walks through the village and up Wolstonbury ('Danny') hill to sing the 17th century *Hymnus Eucharistus* which is followed by the gift of Lowe's Dole, £1 to each boy who had served in chapel during the last year, in the choir, as a sacristan or an organist, from the gift of the first headmaster. More prosaically, the boys then hurry back to school as fast as their legs can carry them to spend the money on sweets in the school tuck shop.

Every religious feast has its food traditions and many of them have been absorbed into the traditions of schools founded in the name of one or other faith. Ascension Day is rather apparently associated with upward flight, suggesting to the leadership of a Christian educational foundation an excuse for a healthy uphill scramble followed by a celebratory communal picnic. Tradition suggests that the business of vertical take-off should be commemorated with feathered food and fowl, pigeon, pheasant or even crow have made their way onto Ascension Day menus. German chefs make bird shaped pastries which sound a good deal more pleasing than crow, even covered with a nice flaky piecrust in a rook pie. Bird pie, including one in which the birds, like the four and 20 blackbirds, remained alive to fly out when the pastry was cut open, was a Tudor and Stuart favourite but one more usually seen at Christmas. There was, may still be, a tradition that some loyal officer of state should send a fully cooked pie containing a great number of birds, four and 20 woodcock for instance, to the monarch at that time of year.

Picnic Crumbs

I don't remember any picnicking attached to the stiff walk up neighbouring Hambledon or Hod hills on Ascension Day when I was at prep school in Dorset. Later, at public school in Wiltshire, we followed a whole school general knowledge test in the morning, which was taken very seriously indeed, with an outing in buses to the Marlborough Downs and a gentler stroll to the 19th century white horse above the village of Alton Barnes. Picnics came always in individual paper bags and held few surprises although they seemed interesting enough in days when school food still meant Heinz style spaghetti in tomato sauce, banana custard and toad in the hole and the dining room had the typical school smell of antique boiled brassicas. Ex-pupils a few years older than me remember special pastries for Ascension Day picnics with circles of red, yellow and green jam, not surprisingly called traffic lights.

Special pastries for Ascension Day in this country, not so far as anyone knows bird-shaped, were called Rammalation Cakes and usually eaten at the end of the ceremony of beating the parish bounds on the Rogation Days immediately preceding Ascension Day in the old church calendar. Rogation days were associated with the blessing of crops and prayers for a good harvest and the cakes were accompanied by Gangen beer. The etymology of both names has been as completely lost as their recipes. I rather doubt that Rammalation Cakes looked like traffic lights but the traffic lights may have had some underlying symbolism, unknown to us but dreamt up in the imagination of our deeply religious and slightly strange headmistress.

Other school picnics, speech days, parents' days and sports days, are part of unchanging traditions of celebration of the lives of long dead founders. Depending on the age of the school, some a lot deader than others. They are often a good enough excuse for pupils to get blind drunk on the vast supplies of alcohol brought by parents keen to get through the whole thing feeling as little pain as possible and can end in recrimination and retribution when things get out of hand. They are also the time when most parents discover that, however grand the school and barring a very few others who are already friends, all the rest are odd, bad or mainly boring. After experiencing about 30 years of such occasions in a great number of schools, I know this to be the case. It is also inevitable that you will suddenly make friends with those you have shunned for years just as your child is leaving. There is comfort in good food as well as alcohol.

My summer school picnic has become as standardised by family demand as the unending cold chicken of travellers' picnics through the years but that does make it very easy too. This is it with the occasional inclusion of an inelegant but good egg mayonnaise without which a picnic is not complete for my husband.

Really good crisps with taramasalata and yoghurt dip; cold asparagus with mayonnaise or vinaigrette; a bowl of cherry tomatoes on their branches; another of cherries or grapes; a great many sticky chipolata sausages, cooked in honey or treacle with grain mustard and packed up in silver foil in plastic boxes wrapped with picnic rugs to arrive still warm; small pieces of chicken marinated overnight in soy, mirin, ginger, garlic, cooked in the oven in the marinade and wrapped like the sausages; lettuce leaves to wrap the teriyaki chicken with cucumber fingers, sliced spring onion and, oddly, much loved *hoisin* sauce; phyllo pasties or samosas of spiced duck or other minced or curried meat; possibly soup, gazpacho or hot tomato, depending on the weather; a ripe brie, butter and a French loaf or two; assorted cakes, biscuits or chocolates, definitely not homemade. Then there are paper plates, paper napkins, plastic glasses in sizes to suit wine or soup, plastic spoons and forks; a handful of proper sharp knives; a corkscrew; a bottle opener; wet wipes; a bin bag and another bag for dirty non-disposables. The food is mostly packed in bowls and dishes balanced in some sort of non-refrigerated box. Things like wine, beer and butter that need to stay cold go in the usual insulated affairs or plastic boxes filled with ice. The drink is champagne, perhaps; the makings of Pimms, probably; and the palest pink wine, definitely; plus lager, coke or lemonade; cider and water.

Constance Spry says that, 'Hungry boys like hot dogs; frankfurters poached in boiling water for seven minutes, drained, and put into a soft fresh roll or bap buttered, lavishly spread with French mustard and given a rub of garlic; or a grilled chipolata in a French roll', so perhaps that is why my sausages always disappear so fast.

Bryanston School Spicy Plum Chutney

900g plums; 450g onions, peeled and finely chopped; 450g sultanas; 900g white granulated sugar; 1.2 litres distilled malt vinegar or wine vinegar; 1 rounded teaspoon ginger; 2 round teaspoons mustard seeds; ½ rounded teaspoon curry powder; ½ rounded teaspoon cinnamon; ½-1 level teaspoon ground cloves; 25g salt.

Stone the plums and chop into 5mm pieces. Put all the ingredients including the plums into a wide stainless-steel pan. Simmer gently over a low-medium heat until the sugar has dissolved and the mixture is soft and pulpy, stirring frequently. Cook uncovered for approximately 1½-2 hours until very thick and dark brown and reduced to about 1/3 of original volume. Stir frequently towards the end of the cooking time to avoid the chutney burning as it becomes more concentrated. Pot in sterilised jars, cover immediately and label. Store in dry, airy cupboard or larder and allow to mature for four weeks before using.

M.F.K. Fisher remembers American school picnics in the late 20s or early 30s for festivals like Easter and Old Girls' Day when the school cook, an otherwise unpleasing character, showed off her remarkable culinary skill to best advantage. She must have been an extraordinary woman who not only fed her charges four times a day 'with probably the best institutional food in America' but also managed to do so under circumstances when normal domestic irritations like flooded basements were overtaken by high drama. Even the head boy committing 'double murder and hara kiri' on Good Friday failed to delay or diminish a good meal.

Old Girls' Day meant wearing gym bloomers without stockings and a lavish picnic on the sea shore below the school in which the most memorable ingredients were 'the hot crisp halves of young chickens, stiff and tempting' eaten in the fingers with abandon and in as great a quantity as anyone could manage.

School picnics also mean packed lunches and, oh dear, what a vexed question they have become now we are so excessively and changeably informed on proper food for growing children. Older books called things like *Healthy Food for Kids* or, supposedly more infant friendly, Winnie the Pooh's 'Healthy Snacks', an oxymoron of a title if ever there was, suggest interesting ways to serve up peanut butter among other healthy options that are now completely banned from class rooms due to ALLERGIES. Peanuts are a regular part of the diet given to undernourished children in developing countries; they are cheap, packed with protein, vitamins and minerals and could be called life rather than deathnuts, which is another name they go by, though it appears to pre-date allergies and anaphylactic shock. The latest view is that the peanuts used in developing countries are the real unprocessed deal and it is in the processing that allergens appear; this probably does not come as a blinding shock to most of us.

Other expectedly healthy foods can also cause anaphylaxis – most nuts; cow's milk; egg; soya; wheat; seeds; seafood; mustard; fish; sulphite food preservatives that are found in foods and drinks from Sauvignon Blanc to sausages and, strangely, celery. Allergies are also caused by meat, sesame seeds, different vegetables and on and on... So, what do you put in a child's packed lunch these days when almost everything that used to be healthy might now make another child ill? No peanut butter, egg, or sardine sandwiches one supposes, not even in gluten free bread, no celery sticks that my children used to eat all the time. According to the books, whatever the food is, it has to be packed in appetising little packages in the Disneyfied lunch box that will make the little darling jump for joy as well as giving it the energy to get through the afternoon.

A 1985 pre-allergy panic book offers savoury and sweet sandwiches full of various nutty mixtures, among other dainty dishes that would keep you up all night making them. Somehow there is no cohesion and no standard dish that might appeal to most children as seems more to be the case in countries with a more clearly defined national cuisine than ours. Maybe I'm wrong, but I doubt any of my children would have eaten a sandwich made of low-fat curd cheese mashed with cold peas and mint and filled with thinly sliced cold lamb, let alone tongue, margarine and redcurrant jelly. More child-pleasing ideas from the same publication, involving the sweet and sticky such as chocolate spread, would no longer be at all the thing during an obesity epidemic and a steady rise in childhood diabetes and I can't say that chocolate spread ever seemed an ideal lunch dish.

This 'Children's Favourite' ticks most of the health and allergen boxes I should imagine, notwithstanding the ketchup, but is it going to be eaten from its small plastic bowl with a snap on lid by some child more interested in play than food?

Children's Favourite

- 2 tablespoons diced cooked chicken
- 1-2 tablespoons cooked peas or green beans
- 1-2 tablespoons cooked sweetcorn or baked beans
- 1 small sliced carrot, cooked or raw
- 1 tablespoon tomato ketchup
- 1 tablespoon plain yoghurt

Mix altogether.

I have unpacked an awful lot of uneaten lunch boxes in my time and I think this might have been in one of them. Perhaps all children now are better brainwashed to eat healthily unless they are the obese ones of course but one can't help but feel that hours spent constructing terribly healthy little bits of this and that are more to make parents feel better than anything else. Really children like food that is quick and easy to eat and tastes right; usually straightforward sandwiches in some hopefully non-allergenic form, fruit ready to eat, carrot sticks maybe, raisins or similar and fruity yoghurts or fromage frais. Depressingly they would probably prefer crisps, chocolate and their sandwich bread white and soggy, whether we like it or not.

School Food

Children's packed lunches in other countries often sound so much better than ours although they too are increasingly adulterated by the crisps and fast food options available all over the world. In Asia particularly, foods that are part of everyday cooking seem to lend themselves well to the packed lunch. Japan children might have *onigiri*, rice balls, or *norimake*, seaweed rolls of rice and something savoury or the same bento boxes as adults. These may take time in the making but will use similar ingredients to those being cooked for the family dinner; rice, omelette strips, cooked meat or fish, cooked or pickled vegetables and umeboshi, Japanese pickled apricot.

Madhur Jaffrey's description of children on a school expedition to the temples at Mahabalipuram in Tamil Nadu eating their packed lunches from banana leaves and tiffin carriers makes one hungry to read it. It somehow sounds so sophisticated and civilised compared with the plastic boxes but these days they have taken over India too.

> 'Having inspected, with required awe, the carved granite temples built at Mahabalipuram on Tamil Nadu's eastern shore some one thousand two hundred years ago, they are about to embark upon the exceedingly pleasant business of eating their lunches.
>
> One girl opens up a newspaper bundle to reveal a second package made out of banana leaf. She smooths out the newspaper with her tiny hands, transforming it into an instant tablecloth. Then she undoes the second package to reveal two spongy *idlis* shaped like small flying saucers. To make them, a batter of ground, parboiled rice and split peas (*urad dal*) was left to ferment overnight. In the morning, when it was a mass of tiny, seething bubbles, it was poured into a whole tree of madeleine-like moulds and steamed. The small, fluffy cakes that formed in the vapour could, of course, have been eaten instantly with a coconut chutney but, for the child going on a trip, they were dipped into oil to prevent them from turning sour in the hot sun and then dipped again into *milagai podi*, a glorious mixture of roasted and coarsely ground seasonings

such as sesame seeds, coriander seeds, red chillies and split peas.

A second child, her braided hair tied up in two loops with crisp ribbons, has opened up her tiffin-carrier and is using a spoon to tuck into yoghurt rice – or curd rice, as they say here when speaking in English. The preparation of this dish has been nothing short of ingenious. In the morning, freshly cooked, slightly soft rice was mixed with milk and a few spoons of yoghurt. Then the combination was seasoned with mustard seeds, *urad dal* and red chillies, popped quickly in hot oil, as well as fresh bits of green coriander, green chillies and ginger. As the child peered at massive elephants carved out of granite rocks or monkeys caught in playful poses on a stone frieze, the contents of her tiffin-carrier were going through a metamorphosis. The same heat that might have soured the first child's *idlis* had precautions not been taken, were working to the benefit of the second child by turning the milk in her container into yoghurt. A dish that was half-prepared when the child left home in the early morning was, by noon, the glorious, cooling, soothing, perky rice salad of the South, called *thayir saadam* in Tamil Nadu and *masuru anna* in Karnataka.' (*A Taste of India*)

The scarcity of interesting food at boarding schools in the past encouraged the creative and the naughty to add excitement by eating the wrong things in the wrong place at the wrong time. Stealing bread to cook over a smoky fire in the woods above the games pitches or, the usual climax to the term at Mallory Towers and other fictional schools, the midnight feast. I remember some very strange ones; purloined champagne that blew its top under the covers of someone's bed, a lot of pink and white sugar mice and slabs of cheddar cheese that were improbably sold by the ounce off an enormous block in the local off licence, our nearest out of bounds shop. Boarders these days are hardly likely to bother with such innocent rule-breaking shenanigans when they have good enough food in dining rooms, sixth form coffee shops, kitchens in their boarding houses and regular supplies of food from local shopping trips and days out. When we were incarcerated juniors, the older girls, who were allowed into the local town, brought back digestive biscuits to sell in the lower school for five pence each, whole Mars bars were worth impossible amounts and were usually profitably sold off in minutely measured slices at more affordable prices.

My son's traditional prep school provided the child actors and the setting for the film, *A Feast at Midnight,* starring Christopher Lee as a vampirish Latin teacher and Robert Hardy as a suitably tweedy headmaster. The arrival of a new boy, Magnus, who detests the all-important team games but loves food, leads to the creation of the 'Scoffers Club' dedicated to the secret cooking of boy fantasy puddings. In a rebellion against the excessively healthy school regime, huge chocolate cakes and crackling crème brulees are constructed in the deserted night-time kitchens using recipes supplied by Magnus' gourmet father. From the child actors' point of view the best part was creeping about their real school at night and the finale, a food fight on a spectacular scale in the school dining room.

The best fictional school feast for me is in *A Little Princess*, Frances Hodgson Burnett's undoubtedly sentimental but quite delicious story of Sara Crewe, whose pampered existence at Miss Minchin's Select Seminary for Young Ladies comes to a dramatic end when her wealthy expatriate father's speculative investment in diamond mines fails and he dies in India of jungle fever. Sara's imagination contrives to transform her new existence of miserable servitude at Miss Minchin's hands and the cold in her dirty garret into the life of a princess imprisoned in the Bastille where she draws her fellow prisoner, Becky, the little scullery maid, into her magical dreams of food, warmth and comfort. The magic begins to come true when another 'Indian Gentleman', Mr Carrisford, moves into the house next door to the seminary with his servant, Ram Dass, to whom Sara speaks in Hindustani, her childhood language, when his monkey escapes across the rooftop into her attic window. Things start to change for Sarah when she falls asleep after a scene with the terrible Miss Minchin, who has caught her remaining friends among the pupils visiting her room.

"'Suppose there was a bright fire in the grate, with lots of little dancing flames,' she murmured. 'Suppose there was a comfortable chair before it – and suppose there was a small table near, with a little hot – hot supper on it. And suppose' – as she drew her thin coverings over her – 'suppose this was a beautiful soft bed, with fleecy blankets and large downy pillows. Suppose – suppose –' and her very weariness was good to her, for her eyes closed and she fell fast asleep.

When she awakened it was rather suddenly, and she did not know that any particular thing had called her out of her sleep. The truth was, however, that it was a sound which had called her back – a real sound – the click of the skylight as it fell in closing after a lithe white figure which slipped through it and crouched down close by upon the slates of the roof – just near enough to see what happened in the attic, but not near enough to be seen.

Of course it was a dream. She felt as if warm, delightful bedclothes were heaped upon her. She could actually *feel* blankets, and when she put out her hand it touched something exactly like a satin-covered-eider-down quilt. She must not awaken from this delight – she must be quite still and make it last.

Her eyes opened in spite of herself. And then she actually smiled – 'Oh I *haven't* awakened, I am dreaming yet.' She knew it must be a dream, for if she were awake such things could not – could not be.

This is what she saw. In the grate there was a glowing, blazing fire; on the hob was a little brass kettle hissing and boiling; spread upon the floor was a thick, warm crimson rug; before the fire a folding-chair, unfolded, and with cushions on it; by the chair a small folding-table, covered with a white cloth, and upon it spread small covered dishes, a cup, a saucer, a teapot; on the bed were new warm coverings and a satin-covered down quilt. At the foot a curious wadded silk robe, a pair of quilted slippers and some books. The room of her dream seemed changed into fairyland.

She took her candle and stole out of her own room and into Becky's, and stood by her bedside.

'Becky, Becky!' she whispered as loudly as she dared. 'Wake up!'

Imagine if you can, what the rest of the evening was like. How they crouched by the fire, which blazed and leaped and made so much of itself in the little grate. How they removed the covers of the dishes and found rich, hot , savoury soup, which was a meal in itself, and sandwiches, and toast and muffins enough for both of them.

It cannot be denied that as they sat before the blazing fire and ate the nourishing, comfortable food, they felt a kind of rapturous awe, and looked into each other's eyes with something like doubt.

'Do you think,' Becky faltered once, in a whisper - 'do you think it could melt away, miss? Hadn't we better be quick?' And she hastily crammed her sandwich into her mouth. If it was only a dream, kitchen manners would be overlooked."

(Frances Hodgson Burnett, *A Little Princess* 1905)

A Finale of Sandwiches and Filling Stuff

In the end a sandwich makes the best and easiest picnic or packed lunch, suiting all circumstances and eventualities with some fitting filling or other. Lord Sandwich's mythical first at the gaming tables; later, more elegant with drinks at the bridge table; the mighty doorsteps of cottage loaf, slab of cheese and dollop of pickle for the outdoor worker; the individually crafted creation of the boutique city sandwich shop eaten at the computer screen; the too cold constructions of supermarkets and coffee shop chains; the smoked salmon in opera or ballet intervals; do-it-yourself baps and rolls for country picnics with ham and rough pâtés; holiday breakfast bacon and mustard; and the unchanging pleasure of elegantly tiny crustless teatime sandwiches, seldom fitted in to hurried daily schedules except as rare hotel or weekend treats. The brown, white, pitta, baguette, organic, gluten free, light as a feather slimming, soda, country, sourdough, ciabatta, walnut, milk, and olive oil bread choices. The no butter, yes butter, margarines and spreads, mayonnaise and mustard decisions to be made. The salad dressed or undressed, the American crammed, the French ham roll, the prosciutto stuck between the teeth, the hatefulness of sweet corn in it all disaster. The honey and the hummus, sardines and salmon paste, dressed crabs and Dublin prawns, with rocket, lettuce, baby spinach and mustard and cress, tomato, not cucumber, soaking through the spongy bread, toasted bread and grilled cheese, topless in Scandinavia, wrapped in South America. You can't go wrong with a sandwich.

'The proper accompaniment of a sandwich is not the schoolboy's ginger beer or railway station coffee, but a glass of champagne, or some of the excellent white French wines which at present are cheaper than beer.

If a busy City millionaire can lunch on sandwiches and desires nothing better, why shouldn't sandwich lunches be popular in Mayfair? There is as much art in making sandwiches as in preparing a French menu, and many hostesses who offer their friends indifferently cooked pretentious lunches would, with far less trouble, gain an epicurean reputation if they were content with the simplicity of wine and sandwiches.'

(Hilda Leyel and Olga Hartley, *The Gentle Art of Cookery*)

'All I shall say, then, is that the food of the perfect picnic should be near the earth and of it, without being lethal or botulistic, should include, crushed between the Stonehenge boulders that sometimes do service for bread, none of those slimy layers of paste like something out of *The Ancient Mariner*.'

(Osbert Sitwell)

Sandwich's Sandwich (The very first)

From *Cookery Recipes by Famous People for Returned British Prisoners of War Association Cookery Book* to which the then Earl of Sandwich contributed this:

Cut two slices of bread of medium thickness, triangular in shape; spread each with butter on one side, putting the buttered sides together. Insert between them a slice of cold meat, beef, mutton, ham, chicken or other bird, or sardine. Add, to taste, a little salt or mustard or sliced pickle – as an alternative or addition mustard, cress or salad. Press firmly together.

A

Asparagus Rolls

Cooked Asparagus tips dipped in Plain Dutch sauce and rolled in thinly sliced buttered wholemeal bread. For the Dutch Sauce: a large gravy spoonful of white sauce heated in a pan with 4 egg yolks, a little grated nutmeg, 2oz butter, salt and pepper; stir briskly on the fire; pass through a hair sieve; keep warm and add a little tarragon vinegar or lemon juice before using. These can be varied with savoury or plain seasoned butters.
(Florence White, *Good Things in England*)

B

Banana Hallucinations (suggested by Claudia Roden)

'As children in Egypt we were amazed to see our English school friends mashing bananas with thick cream and putting them into a sandwich with a very thin layer of strawberry jam'.

Did English children in Egypt really eat these? We used to have plain sliced bananas in brown bread and butter which were delicious.

'Sandwiches for afternoon tea, or any occasion where they will come in contact with gloved fingers, should be left perfectly plain on the outside, but when they may be eaten with a fork some pretty effects may be produced by decorating them with variously-coloured chaudfroid sauces. Or they may be decorated with cold aspic jelly, and garnished with lobster coral, Krona pepper, parsely, cress, small salad, hard-boiled egg, etc'
(Mrs Beeton, *Household Management*)

Eating sandwiches with a fork seems to reduce the whole concept somewhat.

C

Caviare Sandwiches

'Prepare some thin slices of bread, spread them lightly with Russian caviar, sprinkle with lemon-juice and a little cayenne. Have ready an equal number of slice of bread and creamed butter, cover, press lightly together, trim, and cut into square, triangular, or finger-shaped pieces. These sandwiches may be varied by using lobster, prawn, or shrimp butter, any of which flavours combine agreeably with that of caviar.'

(*Mrs Beeton*)

D

Delhi Sandwich (Leyel and Hartley)

'Six anchovies, three sardines, one teaspoonful of chutney, one egg, one ounce of butter, one small teaspoonful of curry powder.

Free the sardines and anchovies from bones. Pound them with the seasonings, the chutney and butter. Beat up the yolk of the egg and stir this in, with a pinch of cayenne. Heat the mixture stirring it into a smooth paste.

This is excellent spread between toast. The toast should be made in rather thick slices, split in two, and the soft sides buttered.'

E

Epicurean Butter

8 anchovy fillets; yolks of 2 hard-boiled eggs; 4oz (115g) softened unsalted butter; ½ teaspoon Dijon mustard; 12 crushed green peppercorns; 2 small gherkins, finely chopped;

1 level teaspoon finely chopped capers; 1 level tablespoon finely chopped chives; 1 level tablespoon finely chopped tarragon or chervil; a squeeze of lemon juice; 8 slices fresh thin wholemeal or white bread from a large loaf.

Blend anchovy fillets in a food processor with the crumbled egg yolks, butter and mustard or pound the ingredients in a bowl. Mix in the peppercorns, gherkins, capers, chives and tarragon. Add lemon juice to taste. Spread on crustless bread slices to make sandwiches.'

(Readers Digest, *Creative Cooking and Entertaining*)

F

Fish Sandwiches

Cut some slices of brown bread and butter and put a layer of nice cold fish. Spread this over with gherkin, then tartar sauce, and over this lay some thin slices of cold hard boiled egg, and a sprinkling of shredded lettuce leaves on top, then press the top slice of bread, and butter well down and cut into diamond shapes.'

(The Anglo-Indian Cuisine)

'Sandwiches of thinnest gruyere between biscuits, or bread spread with green butter are excellent, and this is easily made and welcome in winter and summer, giving variety to the cheese course'

G

Green Butter (Agnes Jekyll, Kitchen Essays)

A ¼lb good fresh butter. A couple of handfuls of spinach, boiled, drained and passed through a hair sieve, the pulp obtained saved in a bowl. Bone and wipe off the oil of 6 anchovies, pass through sieve and save pulp. Mince finely a tablespoonful of capers. Colour the butter first by working in the spinach greening, then add the other ingredients and turn into a block or an attractive small mould, or use for sandwiches after hardening in the ice box.

H

Hard-boiled Eggs

'Hard-boiled eggs would make a good sandwich if it were not for their untidiness in consumption; as it is, an egg in one hand and bread and butter, or a sandwich, in the other is the best way to deal with them. But eggs are very valuable in many of the mixtures for placing between slices of bread and butter.'

(The Pleasures of the Table, Meals Sub-Jove)

Indian Sandwiches

Cut the breast of a roast fowl or pheasant in very small square pieces, also about four ounces of tongue or lean ham, four anchovies washed and filleted; mix well with the chicken, and put it into a stew-pan with two spoonfuls of velouté sauce, a dessert-spoonful of curry paste, half a teaspoonful of chutnee, the juice of half a lemon, and a little salt and pepper. Boil for a few minutes on the stove, mixing well. Have ready prepared some thin slices of bread cut with a circular cutter, as many as you require for your dish, fry them in oil of a bright yellow, drain them on a napkin, and place half of them on a baking-sheet covered with clean paper; spread a thick layer of the above preparation on each, and cover with another crouton. Next grate four ounces of parmesan, cheese, mix it into a paste with butter, divide it into as many parts as there are sandwiches, roll each into a round ball and place one on the top of each sandwich. About ten minutes before serving put them into the oven; let them be thoroughly heated; pass a red hot salamander over them; dish on a napkin and serve.'

(Lady Harriet St Clair, *Dainty Dishes*)

J

Jam

1 kilo strawberries (net weight); 750g sugar; 1dl water.

Put the sugar in a pan with the water; let it dissolve and cook to the ball stage (240° F), taking care to skim well.

Put the strawberries, stalks removed, in the sugar. Keep the pan on the side of the fire for a few minutes.

When the juice from the strawberries has thinned the sugar to a syrupy consistency, drain the fruit through a silk strainer.

Cook the syrup again in the pan until it reaches 240° once more.

Put the strawberries back in the pan and cook for 5 or 6 minutes, just to the point at which the jam reaches the jelling stage (350° F). Finish in the usual way.

(Larousse Gastronomique)

K

Kipper Cheese Paste

As Grouse cheese paste. 'Pound 6 oz of cold grouse debris with the same amount of gruyere cheese, add 2 oz of butter, season with salt and cayenne pepper and pass through the sieve. Finish with two tablespoons of double cream. Should gruyere cheese not be available some new Cheshire or Cheddar may be substituted. You will find that, if you make this paste into a suitable sixed block and keep it in a cold place, you will be able to cut slices from it, arrange them on toast, frill them and serve as an excellent savoury.

(William Heptinstall, *Hors D'Oeuvre and Cold Table*)

L

Lady Llanover's Rice Bread

'In 1867, Lady Llanover writing in Good Cookery gave a detailed description of the preparation of food cooked to be taken on a journey from South Wales to London. For the sandwiches two plump chickens were roasted, and rice bread specially baked the previous day. Lady Llanover held that rice bread was by far the best kind for sandwiches, and preserved the moistness of the chicken meat as well as its own.

Rice is now so expensive that using it for bread can scarcely be called an economy, except in so far as it does give exceptional keeping qualities to the loaf. It is hard to describe the flavour of rice bread: until it has been tried, it is also difficult to believe how delicious it is.'

(Elizabeth David, *English Bread and Yeast Cookery*)

M

Mosaic Sandwiches

Cut heart shapes out of thin slices of white and dark bread trimmed of their crust. Spread half the brown hearts and half the white hearts with butter and filling. Using a tiny heart cutter, cut a small heart from each of the remaining bread hearts and cover the sandwiches, the fillings will show through. Diamonds, stars, circles or any assortment of attractive shapes may be used.

(The Gourmet Cookbook)

N

Nan's Connyonny

'My Nan ate connyonny sandwiches, they were a Liverpool speciality, condensed milk spread between two slices of bread. She gave us sugar sandwiches and called a packed lunch a carryon. We ate chip butties too – still do sometimes and food of any sort was known as scran.'

(Liz from Liverpool)

O

Offula

The sandwich was not first hit upon by the earl in the reign of George III, as the Romans were very fond of sandwiches, called by them, *offula*.

'It is curious to think of this dashing edible, the sustenance of lords at their dice coming to the support nowadays of school treats, business girls, stock-jobbers, and debutantes dewy with primal innocence. But happily few are aware of its origin, and fewer still brood upon its inventor. He walked with a shamble, he was supremely unlucky at cards, and denied by Fate even the compensatory good fortune in love. Miss Ray, his delightful actress mistress, was shot as she left her theatre one night by an amorous clergyman. I know, as has been explained in another place, nothing whatever about the Romans; therefore I begin and end my introduction of the sandwich with this brief note upon its eponym, and ignore the repulsively named offula as entirely as I may.'

(Helen Simpson, *The Cold Table*)

P

Pumpkin and Tomato Chutney

'It is not generally known that pumpkin can make an excellent chutney, rich and dark. The recipe below produces a mixture with a taste which is spicy but not too sharp; the pumpkin slices retain something of their shape, and shine translucently through the glass jars.

Ingredients are a 2½ lb piece of pumpkin (gross weight), 1lb of ripe tomatoes, ½lb onions, 2oz. of sultanas, ¾lb each of soft dark brown sugar and white caster sugar, 2 tablespoons of salt, 2 scant teaspoons each of ground ginger, black peppercorns and allspice berries, 2 cloves of garlic, 1¼ pints of white, red or rosé wine vinegar or cider vinegar.

Peel the pumpkin, discard the seed and the cottony centre. Slice, then cut into pieces roughly 2 inches wide and long and ½ inch thick. Pour boiling water over the tomatoes, skin and slice them. Peel and slice the onions and the garlic.

Put all solid ingredients, including spices (crush the peppercorns and allspice berries in a mortar) and sugar, in your preserving pan. (For chutneys always use heavy aluminium, never untinned copper jam pans.) Add vinegar. Bring gently to the boil, and then cook steadily, but not at a gallop until the mixture is jammy. Skim from time to time, and towards the end of the cooking, which will take altogether about 50 minutes, stir very frequently. Chutney can be a disastrous sticker if you don't give it your full attention during the final stages.

This is a long-keeping chutney, but like most chutneys, it is best if cooked to a moderate set only; in other words it should still be a little bit runny; if too solid it will quickly dry up.

Ladle into pots, which should be filled right to the brim. When cold cover with rounds of waxed paper, and then with Porosan skin or a double layer of thick greaseproof paper. Transparent covers which let in the light are not suitable for chutney.

The yield from these quantities will be approximately 3½lb; and although it may be a little more extravagant as regards fuel and materials, I find chutney cooked in small batches more satisfactory than when produced on a large scale.'

(Elizabeth David, *Spices, Salt and Aromatics in the English Kitchen*)

Q

Quince Paste (Dulce de Membrillo)

Peel and core 2kg quinces. Roughly chop the flesh and put it in a heavy pan with the water. Bring the water to the boil, turn down to a simmer, cover and leave to cook for 30 minutes. At the end of this time you will have purée. Process or sieve to remove lumps. Weigh the purée and stir in 250g of sugar per 500g of pulp.

Return the sugared pulp to the pan and simmer for 45 minutes uncovered. At the end of this time pour the mixture into a lightly greased oblong baking tray, to the depth of about 2.5cm. Leave to cool and when it is completely cold cut into squares. Store in a tin wrapped in greaseproof paper. (Quince, Damson and other fruit cheeses were well known in old English cookery but the Moorish or Spanish versions are the ones we see now to be eaten with hard cheese, especially Spanish Manchego.)

(Sarah Woodward, *Moorish Food*)

R

Reality Sandwiches

> *On Burrough's Work*
> *The method must be purest meat*
> *and no symbolic dressing,*
> *actual visions and actual prisons*
> *as seen then and now*
>
> *Prisons and vision presented*
> *with rare descriptions*
> *corresponding exactly to those*
> *of Alcatraz and Rose*
>
> *A naked lunch is natural to us*
> *we eat reality sandwiches.*
> *But allegories are so much lettuce.*
> *Don't hide the madness.*
> San Jose 1954
> (Allen Ginsberg, *Reality Sandwiches*)

S

Soho Sandwiches

Ingredients: White bread; powdered Parmesan cheese; butter; Italian vermouth.

Toast on one side only very thin slices of bread. Make a paste of the powdered Parmesan and vermouth. Butter the untoasted side of the bread and spread the paste on this. Put two pieces together or cover the paste with crisp salted potato crisps.

Note. The cheese must be powdered not merely grated (*The Cold Table*)

En Fin

I had set out in this book to cover stories of picnics and outdoor eating as comprehensively as I could but even with so long a list of wonderful and extraordinary sources and contributors, I admit defeat. With every book, new or old, I now pick up, another alfresco scene leaps from the pages with ambience, food and drink perfectly pictured and lusciously described, demanding my attention and inclusion amongst the others. What indeed to do? These picnics, however many they have become, were neither a vocation nor meant to become an everlasting occupation but only in the end a personal selection to share from the bottomless supply of remembered frippery picnic amusements occasionally spiced with more dramatic tales of life, death and adventure. Many of the stories were lost in their own time in the pages of the old books that have so appealed to me since childhood, many of the recipes too of course, especially those that appear so unappealing to contemporary tastes.

The food we eat indoors as well as out will change faster this century than ever before as science and climate change play a push-me-pull-you game with the problems and shortages of high population and radical weather. All our food may become freeze-dried like space food or sealed packets of extruded nuts and beans perfectly balanced for optimum nutrition like the extraordinary pulpy nut that now saves lives among malnourished children in the hungriest parts of the world, or, in the case of the rich and fat, to avoid obesity, as well as for cost and ease of distribution. Everything we eat may become a desiccated picnic with no cooking involved and an endless supply of pre-packed, identical vitamin balanced foods, prescribed and created in a laboratory with no scope for imagination, conversation or differing tastes.

Picnic Crumbs

It is an altogether depressing prospect when you think of the varieties of food and venues for its consumption that appear in so many different memories in a book describing only or mainly portable eating possibilities, even those that sound most unappetising. Until food really is only human fuel, I would rather, at the last, hope that this picnic of other people's picnics might be considered an *amuse guele* to an apparently unending menu of outdoor plans and provisions, picnic tales and tastes, at least for those not yet suffering terminal alfresco indigestion. I think all these bits and pieces of my own and other people's picnics, packed lunches and provisions have had that effect on me and at the very end I will leave the foie gras and lobster, even the sticky sausages and simple salads and settle for a perfectly simple egg sandwich for my last picnic, wherever and whenever that happens to be.

Bibliography

Del Bene, Terry Alan, *The Donner Party Cookbook: A Guide to Survival on the Hastings Cutoff*, Quality Books, USA, 2003.

Downey, Andrew (Ed.) *Cookery Recipes by Famous People for Returned British Prisoners of War Association Cookery Book,* Arthur Barker, London, 1950.

Durrell, Gerald, *Fillets of Plaice,* Viking, 1971.

Eden, Emily, *Up the Country: Scenes and Characteristics of Hindostan,* R. Bentley, 1867.

Eden, Frederic, *The Nile without a Dragoman,* H.S. King & Co., London, 1871.

Ehrman, John W., *Notes on Aromatic Sulphuric Acid and Confection of Senna,* The American Journal of Pharmacy, Vol. XLIII, 1871.

Esdaille, Charles, *The Peninsular War,* Allen Lane, London, 2002.

Farley, John, *The London Art of Cookery and Domestic Housekeeper's Complete Assistant,* 1787.

Field, Michael & Frances, *A Quintet of Cuisines,* Time-Life International, Netherlands, 1977.

Fiennes, Ralph, *Mind Over Matter,* Arrow, London, 1999.

Fisher, M.F.K., *The Gastronomical Me, An Alphabet for Gourmets, Serve it Forth, Consider the Oyster,* republished in *The Art of Cooking,* 50th Anniversary Edition, Wiley Publishing Inc, NY, 2004.

Fitzgibbon, Theodore, *The Pleasures of the Table,* OUP, Oxford, 1981, *Memorandum for the Guidance of Pursers and Stewards-in-Charge on Victualling and Management,* P & O Company, 1908.

Fleming, Peter, *One's Company: A Journey to China,* Cape, 1934.

Forster, E.M., *A Passage to India,* 1924.

Fraser, Flora, adapted *Diaries of Maud Berkeley,* Secker & Warburg, London, 1985.

Fuller, Thomas, *Pharmacopoeia Extemporanea,* London, 1710.

Ginsburg, Allen, *Reality Sandwiches,* City Lights Books, San Francisco, 1966.

Gordon, Constance Eveline, *The Anglo-Indian Cuisine,* A.J. Combridge and Co, Bombay, 1904.

Graham, G, *Life in the Mofussil: or, The Civilian in Lower Bengal,* C.K. Paul & Co, London, 1878.

Groden, Leo, *My Royal Cookbook,* typescript, 1962-1964.

Hall, Miranda, *Packed Lunches and Picnics,* Judy Piatkus Ltd., London, 1985.

Hanbury Tenison, Marika, *First Catch Your Crocodile,* published in *The Sunday Telegraph Cookbook,* Granada, London, 1980.

Hare, Ensign William, Photocopied typescript memoirs of Ensign William Henry Hare, 51st (2nd Yorkshire, West Riding) Regiment of Foot, 1868. Archives of National Army Museum.

Heptinstall, William, *Hors D'Oeuvre and Cold Table, A Book of Tried and Trusted Methods,* Faber & Faber Ltd. London, 1959.

Herzog, Maurice, *Annapurna,* Jonathan Cape, London, 1952.

Heyerdahl, Thor, *The Kon-Tiki Expedition,* Allen & Unwin, 1964.

Hillyard, Cdr. G.W., *Ideal Shipmate,* Memoir, (quoted in *King George V,* Kenneth Rose, Macmillan, London, 1983).

Hodgson Burnett, Frances, *A Little Princess,* 1905.

Houlston & Wright, *Enquire Within Upon Everything,* London, 1867.

Hull, Edmund C.P., *The European in India or, Anglo-Indian's Vade Mecum,* Henry S. King & Co, London, 1872.

Hume, Rosemary, *Party Food and Drink,* Chatto & Windus, London, 1950.

Jaffrey, Madhur, *A Taste of India,* Pavilion Books, London, 1983.

Jefferies, Richard, *The Life of the Fields,* London, 1893.

Jekyll, Agnes, *Kitchen Essays,* Thomas Nelson & Sons, London, 1922.

Jerome K Jerome, *Three Men in a Boat,* Arrowsmith, London, 1889.

Bibliography

Wodehouse, P G, *Jeeves and the Old School Chum,* quoted in Kent, Elizabeth, *Picnic Basket,* Fontana, London, 1978.

Woodward, Sarah, *Moorish Food,* Kyle Cathie Ltd., London, 1998 .

Wooler, Neil, *Dinner in the Diner: The History of Railway Catering,* David & Charles, 1987.

Young, Donald (Ed.), *The Search for the Source of the Nile,* Correspondence between Captain Richard Burton and Captain John Speke, The Roxburghe Club, London, 1999.